DEALING WITH IT

My story of overcoming abuse and learning to live a life

Donna Taylor

Copyright © 2023 Donna Taylor

All rights reserved

The characters and events portrayed in this book are fictitious. Any similarity to real persons, living or dead, is coincidental and not intended by the author.

No part of this book may be reproduced, or stored in a retrieval system, or transmitted in any form or by any means, electronic, mechanical, photocopying, recording, or otherwise, without express written permission of the publisher.

ISBN-13: 9798376047385
ISBN-10: 1477123456

Cover design by: Danny Cook
Library of Congress Control Number: 2018675309
Printed in the United States of America
and the United Kingdom

Dedications & Acknowledgements
Firstly, I want to dedicate this to my mum. Some of this is as much her story as it is mine. You've been incredibly strong Mam; I just wish you could see it for yourself. I love you so very much, thank you for your support, your understanding and for always, always having my back!

Secondly, to Terry, you came into my life when I was still trying to put myself back together and you have been so incredibly understanding and supportive. You've given me the courage to work towards what I want and to be who I am and loved me even on my bad days. I feel proud to be with you and I look forward to building our lives together. All my love

My friend Sam, you've been telling me since we first met that I should write my story, well it took me a few years, but it is finally done! Thank you for your friendship, advice, and knowledge about this process and more. Your suggestions have been invaluable, and I count myself lucky to have you as a friend and calling me out on my limiting beliefs and general shit on occasions!

This book wouldn't have been able to go ahead without the help of some very special people who contributed to the crowd-funding campaign to publish it. My absolute heartfelt thanks go to you all and the messages that I have received from some of you showing your support and kindness have moved me to tears!
Sending special thanks to: Yvonne Woodgate, Samantha Houghton, Gary Hancox, Karen Randall, Diana Georgescu, Muriel Russell, Dawn

Brown, Richard Lambe

And finally, a huge thanks go to my editor, Tiffany Hepworth and my cover designer, Danny Cook. Without you two, this book would never have gotten across the line.

Chapter One – My Dad, My hardest relationship

The problem was that dad liked a drink and to gamble. As it was the 80s, life for many families was that the women stayed at home and the men were the breadwinners. My dad, Tony, was a painter and decorator and mum, Yvonne, was a housewife. His gambling habit was mostly horse racing, the pools and spot the ball. But nevertheless, he made it difficult to put food on the table and keep our bills paid! He very rarely won; it had become a joke in the family that he usually bet on the donkey trailing behind at the back of the race! Unfortunately, dad on a losing streak was pretty unbearable and usually led to more drinking. That then became violence and a million miles away from the charming older man, of seventeen years her senior, that my mum thought she was marrying in the November of 1980!

I was born in Leicester the following year. During my early years, when I could be considered cute and had to rely on my parents for my every need, dad was reasonably attentive. In fact, I appeared to be a real daddy's girl. There was the one time that he left me at the local launderette though. When he returned home without me, mum had to point out that he didn't have me with him so sent him back. Luckily, I was quite happy and safe on the manager's knee when he returned. Mum has told me since that she was less than impressed, and yes, dad had been in the pub that day which wasn't a surprise!

When I reached the age of three, my brother Terence (Tez) came along. Dad was forty-four years of age with two bundles of joy, one with an especially powerful cry! Dad wasn't particularly good with kids from what I remember and preferred that we were seen but not heard. I don't know where he got this idea from! Dad was by this point, beginning to develop arthritis in his knees. Not that this should excuse his behaviour in the slightest, but when I was about four years old, there were two incidents that stuck in my mind. I can't remember which one of these came first but here we go!

My family and I were in a café after a shopping trip in Leicester City Centre as mum and dad wanted a cup of tea. Dad asked me if I would like a cake, now me being only four years old, pointed to the most colourful cake on the shelf. It was bright yellow! When dad had paid for everything and brought it over to our table, I went to take a bite. It was horrible so I threw it back onto its plate, shouting that I didn't like it. Within seconds, I thought that my head was going to come off my shoulders! Dad had given me a huge slap across my face shouting words to the effect of "I paid good fucking money for that cake, now eat it!"

I felt people looking at me and I wanted the ground to swallow me up. My eyes began to water, and I dissolved into sobs. It became very apparent that I was not going to eat the cake, which I now know was a custard tart. Mum comforted me and dad took it off the plate and stuck it in his mouth and ate it in three mouthfuls. I still honestly can't bear custard tarts or anything involving cold custard to this day, and I still get shivers at recalling this story!

The second incident took place back at home when I was only four. We lived in a house only five doors away from my dad's mum, my Nanna Taylor. She becomes an important part of our story later on. As I walked down the stairs, I imagined that I was floating down them - I did that a lot. I heard mum and dad arguing, which was not uncommon to be fair. I can't remember what was being said but from my vantage point on the stairs, I saw dad hit mum across the face, the way that he did with me when we were in the café. I ran down the stairs to mum in tears, pleading as to why my daddy had hit my mummy like that? That ended the argument, but later, I was being naughty, and mum told me off. Little me, decided that I was not having any of that, so I smacked her around the face! Poor mum had to sit me down and explain that it's not kind or right to smack people. My little person response was "but daddy did it and you two love each other, so how did I do wrong?"

Mum had to tell me that she loved daddy too but his smacking her was wrong and people shouldn't smack in an argument. I nodded that I understood, my eyes still filled with tears, and I told mum that I was sorry for hurting her.

I spent years in the belief that my younger brother had been spared the same treatment from dad that mum and I regularly received. But I recently learned from mum's diaries that this wasn't the case. He didn't receive quite as many pastings as we did but I'm sure it was just as frightening for him as he was three years younger than me.

There was another incident a little later in my childhood, I think that I was about six years old by this point. I was, and still can be, strong willed at times. On this occasion, I was absolutely determined that I was going to wear my school jumper and not the cardigan for some reason. When I couldn't find it, I started to tear my bedroom apart while heavily crying, probably in sheer anger. Dad came into my bedroom, carrying a cup of coffee. He saw what I was doing, shouted at me and threw his coffee over me. I think that it was cold as I don't recall being burnt but it did nothing to calm me down or stop me crying! Mum came in and shouted at dad when she realised what he had done. She calmed me down enough to get me off to school or at least get me out of that house for the day!

I always craved my dad's love, but he would come in drunk, after visiting the pub after work or just because he wanted a drink, and he wasn't working. I would run to him, full of smiles and enthusiasm and I would either be ignored as he stalked past me with a face like thunder, or he would smack me out of his way. If he hadn't hurt me, I would just return to what I was doing feeling upset.

To understand my dad's temper, I have to introduce his mum, my Nanna Taylor into the mix. She was a tyrant, and it is easy to see where dad's temper came from. She was a very small woman and only weighed about six stone, I swear! My dad's brother, Uncle Roy, lived with Nanna, and he bore the brunt of her temper it would seem. I always felt sorry for Roy. He had been in the Army in his younger years, and I don't know if he had suffered an injury, but he was considered to be a bit 'slow' by 1980s standards. In truth, I think that he was left with learning difficulties but coping on his own would probably have been difficult. If he had been alive today, there would have been so much more help available, and he would probably have had a good life!

However, on one particular day, Nanna wanted Roy to go and buy some toilet rolls. Mum and I were visiting, I was only about five. Roy returned with the toilet rolls and Nanna went into the Kitchen where Roy was unpacking the other bits of shopping that he had purchased for her. The next thing that mum and I knew, was the sound of loud clattering coming from the kitchen and Nanna shouting at Roy. Nanna was actually throwing saucepans at Roy because the toilet rolls were green! She only stopped when mum walked into the kitchen. Poor Roy didn't utter a peep and there was no reaction on his face from what I recall as he went upstairs to his bedroom. This clearly wasn't the first occurrence of my Nan's temper!

Sadly, Roy had an accident in his bedroom in early 1988 and later died of a brain haemorrhage early in April of that year. He never really recovered during his time in hospital despite everything that the doctors and nurses tried to do for him. When Roy died, dad's violence, narcissism and need to control all of our behaviour increased rapidly.

Up until the age of five, I lived only five doors away from my Nanna Taylor. We did spend nine months living in a maisonette in the South of Leicester, only a twenty-minute bus ride away from my Nan, but we moved to the North of Leicester when I was about 6 and a half years old. Having spoken to my mum about her relationship with her mother-in-law, it is clear that she was not happy living so close to Nanna with her temper and the clear hold she had over dad. However, from mum's diaries and her meticulous record keeping of who she had borrowed money from and paid back, it is clear that despite that difficult relationship, it was Nanna who kept us fed and clothed on a regular basis. Due to dad's ineptitude with money and his drinking and gambling, Nanna was our weekly bank. It is noted in mum's diaries that she was displeased with the regular lending, but she did it anyway.

Following the move to North Leicester and subsequently Roy's death, dad desperately wanted to move back to South Leicester. According to mum's diaries, there were many, many arguments, threats, and general violent behaviours in relation to this. By January of 1991 and thanks to conversations with local friends, mum had reached the end of her tether! Mum called social services who agreed to house us temporarily in a bed and breakfast on the edge of Leicester City Centre. One Saturday morning, dad had gone to visit Nanna Taylor alone. Whilst he was gone, mum packed as much of our stuff into bin bags and then we left in a taxi.

When we arrived, we were taken upstairs to the largest room on the top floor. It was actually huge with a double bed, two single beds and a sink with a mirror above it. There was a shared bathroom and kitchen next door, but we were told there was only one other person on that floor, and they were rarely around. I actually really liked this place - dad wasn't around. Being able to order breakfast in the mornings downstairs was a real treat! We were the only young kids, so Tez and I were quite spoilt by the staff. There was a security guard with a beautiful Alsatian/German Shepherd called King. He was huge but such a placid dog. His owner did tell my mum that if King was given the right command, he immediately went into protection mode and the wrong person would not get into the building. That made me feel safe. The owners of the hotel had a grandson and when he visited, he performed magic tricks in the lounge downstairs. We were only there for about ten days, but I felt safe and carefree for the first time in a long time, and I was only nine at this point!

The peaceful feeling wasn't to last however as mum still kept in touch with dad using the phone box down the road. Eventually, she agreed that we would meet up with him in Loughborough, mum did not want dad knowing that we were staying in Leicester City Centre. I never felt at ease meeting up with dad, but we did meet up with him a few more times again away from Leicester City Centre. Tez was always excited to see dad though, he was only six, and one day he blurted out where we were staying. The game was up.

Dad had been slowly turning on the charm with mum, making promises and she had begun to thaw, that much was easy to see! So, we moved back home and refilled our wardrobes and chest of drawers with our clothes from the black bags that we had left with. Of course, the promises that dad had made to mum didn't last. By April 1991, dad had resorted to making threats again and he stepped up his campaign to 'persuade' mum to move.

When we moved into our house in North Leicester, there was a full-size swing frame in the garden. Dad had repainted it for us and varnished the wooden seats. I loved it; it was my favourite thing in the world at the time! I would swing as high as I could and one day, I managed to make myself sick because I went too high. Luckily dad wasn't at home, or I would have faced a slap for being so stupid! But, during a particular argument, dad told mum that if she didn't agree to move then things "were going to get comical." I can picture him saying this through gritted teeth as he often did when he was angry.

He then proceeded to go to the shed and got his hacksaw out. The next thing mum and I knew, he was sawing into the swing frame! Within less than an hour, my favourite thing had gone! I was distraught. Dad came back into the house and his argument with mum continued. I went upstairs to my room in tears and closed the bedroom door and put my toy pram across the door. I was too old for the pram, and I hated dolls, but it sat nicely under my bedroom handle so no one could get in. Dad had never tried to barge into my room, but I needed to feel safe from him.

By the end of that April, things had truly reached a head. Mum and dad had been arguing and I had gone to bed, but I heard mum's cries from the kitchen. I was too terrified to move but too terrified to sleep. Mum came into my bedroom with tears streaming down her face. She had her nightdress and her dressing gown in her hand. She brought some bedding in and made her bed on the floor next to mine. "*This is bad*" I thought to myself as she went to the bathroom to change. Mum came back in, and she had just closed my bedroom door when we heard clattering outside my door. Mum put her finger over her lips to signal me to keep quiet. The clattering stopped and we both barely moved for a couple of minutes in case it caused dad to come in. Slowly and quietly, mum opened the door, piled up behind the door were various items including the tall bathroom bin. Dad had put them there to alert him if we got up in the night. I heard mum whisper "the bastard has barricaded us in."

Silent tears fell down my face, I didn't know what this all meant, but I was afraid! Mum hugged me and wiped my tears away, she whispered to me to go to sleep and settle down and she did the same. I slept fitfully, I'm not sure if mum slept that night in all honesty, I suspect not.

The next morning, mum was already awake, she whispered to me to stay quiet and to stay in my room for a bit. I did as I was told. I could hear dad in the kitchen which was directly below my bedroom, and I was afraid of what he would do when we got up. I must have dozed off again when mum woke me up. I sat up as mum sat on my bed.

"I've told your dad that you're going on a school trip and that you have to go" she said firmly.

I was puzzled and my face must have showed it because she continued:

"I know you don't have a school trip but you're not going to school. You're going to go to my friend Shirley's round the corner and wait for me there, okay?"

I nodded slowly, still not quite sure what was going on, but if it meant getting away from my dad, I would do anything! Mum told me to go and get washed so I got out of bed and when I opened the door, I could see the big bathroom bin, the cane laundry hamper, and various other things on the landing. These were clearly what dad had used to 'barricade' mum and I in my bedroom the night before!

When I returned to my bedroom, mum was there holding a note in her hand. She told me which trousers to wear because they had a back pocket. I must have still had a confused look on my face as I was dressing, and mum explained:

"I'm putting this note in your right back pocket. Now when it's time to go to school, I want you to walk round to Shirley's house, you remember where she lives don't you?"

I nodded as mum continued "when you get there and you get into the house, you tell her that I am coming round as soon as I can and that there is a note in your back pocket that she has to read okay?"

I nodded again, noticing the desperation in her eyes.

"Don't mention this to your dad at all, as far as he is concerned, you're going to the zoo. Can you do all that for me?" She asked.

I threw my arms around her trying to hold back tears. Lying was wrong I knew that, but I knew something bad would happen if I told dad the truth of where I was really going. I knew he didn't like Mum's friends and I could still feel a bad atmosphere in the house. I went downstairs to get breakfast, conscious of the note in my back pocket and hoping that it didn't poke out in front of dad.

I ate my breakfast quietly, I think Tez was still in bed, he clearly wasn't going to school today. Dad marched into the living room, "I'm taking Tez up to my mother's for the day" he announced and turned on his heel and walked out.

I looked at mum and she was gripping onto her teacup with both hands.

"Well, that's me told, ain't it?" She said quietly.

I finished my breakfast, and I could hear Tez moving around upstairs. Mum took my empty breakfast bowl into the kitchen, then I sat on the settee feeling a bit numb and unsure what to do next. mum came back in holding my school bag and my coat.

"Right, it's time you went to call for your mate and get to school. I've put an apple and some crisps in your bag to share out when you get to the zoo."

Mum's face was expressionless as she helped me get my coat on. She hugged me close and whispered in my ear "get to Shirley's and I will see you there soon."

I held onto her for a second longer before I let go, mum opened the door, and I took a breath as I walked out. Mum waved at me as I turned round "have a lovely time at the zoo and I will see you later" she called out, almost a little bit too loud.

I smiled and waved back, and I saw her close the door, so I turned around and breathed out. I walked at a faster speed than usual; Shirley's house was only around the corner. I knocked on her door fast and hard and as Shirley opened it, I almost fell through the door.

"Donna, what's up, where's your mam?" she asked with surprise.

By this point, I'd begun to feel a bit teary, and she noticed. She bent down to caringly wipe my tears away. I couldn't keep the emotion out of my voice as I spoke "mum's coming round as soon as she can, there's a note for you in my back pocket."

Shirley hugged me as she retrieved the note from my pocket, her face darkened as she read it. Shirley let me go and took me into her living room, guided me to the sofa and opened my school bag. She found my latest reading book from school and passed it to me "now I'm going out for five minutes to walk the lads to the top of the alley near the school and then I will be back. Will you be okay to read that until I get back?" Shirley asked brightly.

I smiled and nodded, I enjoyed reading and I liked Shirley's big comfy sofa. I sat back and settled in to read. As Shirley was leaving with her lads, I heard them asking what I was doing there but then the door closed before I heard Shirley's reply. A few minutes later, Shirley burst through the door. I had gotten into my book, so I jumped slightly. She offered to make us both a cup of tea and I nodded in agreement.

A couple of minutes later, while Shirley was still in the kitchen, someone knocked the door. I heard Shirley open it and then I heard the familiar voice of my mum but with a slight tone of desperation "is Donna here?"

I heard Shirley confirm that I was, and she beckoned her in. Mum strode into Shirley's living room holding her arms out to me. I jumped off the sofa and ran to her for a hug, feeling the relief that she had made it. I sat back down, and

Shirley brought my cup of tea in, and then mum and Shirley went into the kitchen to talk whilst drinking their tea. I heard them talking in hushed tones. I tuned them out and went back to my book.

A while later, mum and Shirley came back into the living room. Mum sat herself next to me and I put my book down. I sensed that mum wanted to talk to me, as I looked at her, I realised for the first time that day that she had a serious looking bruise on one side of her mouth. "You know I ended up sleeping in your room last night, right?" I nodded, unable to keep my eyes off of her bruise.

Mum continued "well last night, your dad hurt me and for the last time - Shirley has got us an appointment with a solicitor for later this morning."

I swallowed slowly as I looked at mum "did dad give you that bruise?" I asked.

Mum nodded and explained how dad had grabbed her by the side of the mouth and pulled her around the kitchen. My eyes were wide as I tried to hold the tears back and then I realised that Tez was still with dad. "What about Tez - will he be safe with dad?"

The fear was evident in my voice. Mum was quiet for a second as she thought. "He's gone to your Nan's for the day. Tez will be fine as long as he behaves."

I kept my doubts about the chances of that to myself! Although Tez was the apple of my dad's eye and Nanna Taylor adored him, so he was likely to be fine as he got away with much more than I ever did!

We all readied ourselves and made our way into Leicester City Centre on the bus. Shirley joined us for moral support. The solicitors were on the outskirts of the City Centre. We waited in the waiting room for a couple of minutes and then we were called into the office of a bearded, bespectacled man called Mr Bergman. Apparently, he was to be mum's solicitor. We all took a seat opposite Mr Bergman and mum relayed what had happened and why we were in his office.

He listened quietly before telling mum the details of what he could do. I don't quite remember the details but in essence, a restraining order would be applied for an injunction to remove dad from the house, a temporary custody order would be applied for to grant mum full custody of my brother and I, and when the time was right, divorce proceedings would be issued.

Mum filled in lots of forms and signed lots of documents. Mr Bergman told us that he had arranged an emergency appointment at the Family Court for that afternoon. Mum and Shirley decided that we should go for a cup of tea and a bite to eat in the meantime but not before getting a note pad and some pencils for me. I couldn't, and still can't draw, but I did like to doodle and write.

Before we attended the Family Court, mum had to go to the building across the road to complete her application for legal aid. The lady at reception gave mum a printout of what to say whilst she had her hand on the Bible and that was it! I never have understood this practise, I didn't find religion growing up and I am waiting for someone to have a genius moment and provide a suitable alternative!

We crossed the road and entered the Family Court building. A small boxy lift took us up to the correct floor. Mr Bergman was there, and we took a seat in a waiting room. Mum's name was called. I stood up and mum told me that I should stay in the waiting room and maybe draw in my new notebook. I sat down feeling a bit put out. I had been at her side through everything and heard everything and now mum had decided that I shouldn't be in the courtroom? I didn't feel like your average nine-year-old anymore and I wanted to know what was going on!

Mum and Shirley returned to the waiting room sometime later. I didn't like being in there and the receptionist had given me a few funny looks. I asked mum what was going to happen now. Mum told me that she had been granted temporary full custody of me and my brother. I'm not sure at what point I started to understand legal language, but I was always told that I had an above average reading age! Mum also told me that a court bailiff would deliver an envelope to our house and dad had to leave the house by 8pm that evening and that he wasn't to come within a certain distance of us until the next time mum went to Court.

I felt all over the place and felt a need to get 'through' the situation and deal with the consequences afterwards. We caught the bus home, and we went to another of mum's friends, Val, who lived at the end of our road. She had a son who was in my brother's class at school.

Val greeted us warmly and made us all some tea. At some point, my Nanna Brown (my mother's mum) and my Uncle Derek arrived. I began to feel a sense of urgency for some reason. A court bailiff knocked on the door, he told mum that he had delivered the letter to dad and had spoken to him through the letterbox because he refused to open the door after swearing at him. That was typical of my dad, he didn't take kindly to authority figures nor being told what to do. He had been made aware of the 8pm deadline and so we just had to wait for him to bring my brother to Val's where we were waiting and leave the house with his belongings.

The wait felt like forever, but shortly before the deadline there was a knock at the door and mum decided to answer it. Dad was standing there with my brother. Tez came into the house, mum and dad spoke as I watched TV. I heard mum shout my name and I went to the door to say goodbye to my dad. Mum left us and went back into the house. He had a large bag at his feet, I didn't really know what to say to him, but I knew that I was glad that he was leaving. He had hurt my mum; he'd hurt me, and my brother and I needed it all to stop. I told him that I would see him soon and kissed his cheek and went back into the house. Everyone was in the living room, and I actually did a little jump and a whoop for joy! I was both relieved and excited by what was to be a new life chapter.

Mum finally closed the door and came back into the living room, Tez had gone upstairs to play on his friend's computer and seemed to be okay. Mum had tears in her eyes, so Nanna gave her a hug. The sense of elation I felt was huge - I wasn't going to be scared all the time anymore. Oh, how a childish mind works and that sense of optimism!

Eventually, we went home, and Nanna and Derek joined us. The adults did a quick check around the house, to check for damage or if anything obvious was missing. All was okay. Tez and I got ready for bed, while Nanna and Derek stayed chatting with mum until late. The day had caught up with me, so I slept pretty well.

Life for the next few days became a new kind of normal, I guess. It was back to school for me and my brother. The school were informed about what had happened with dad. My teacher, Mr Webster, kept a special eye on me. My classroom was quite large with a reading corner that had two sofas. He knew how much I enjoyed reading, so at lunchtimes and break times, if I didn't want to go into the playground, he let me read on the sofas instead. I quite enjoyed this little privilege, and the classroom was lovely and quiet, so I did it a lot for a good few weeks. Of course, it had started to filter through to the other kids about what had happened with my dad. I didn't know what to say or how to talk about it, so I preferred to read my books. Child therapy wasn't a hot topic in the 1990s like it is now!

A few days after dad had left the house was the weekend. Mum announced on the Saturday, that we were going to meet dad in the town centre. We had spoken to him on the phone a few times. I was still at a loss on what to say to dad and that never really changed to be fair!

We met dad at the Clock Tower in town - the meeting place in Leicester City Centre. We went to a café, and we had a walk around town. There was a lot of small talk. Tez was more enthusiastic as he always had a better relationship with dad than I did. Dad had started to turn on the charm with mum again and he got the bus back home with us. I wanted to ask mum how the injunction would be affected because I knew that it was still in effect, but I didn't. Dad stayed with us for about four days. There were no incidents and dad was being 'nice.' I still felt like I was treading on eggshells. I was only nine years old, and I had already lost trust in my dad! I didn't know what to make of dad being so 'normal' and I was fairly sure that he couldn't keep it up and I wanted mum to wake up!

Dad went back to Nanna Taylor's house for another week and then he came back home to us. Again, things were nice. He and Mum were getting on and they were being affectionate, but I was still waiting for the other shoe to drop! I don't remember exactly how or when it came about but a court bailiff was 'allegedly' following mum and dad to make sure that he was abiding by the injunction. Dad began to fall apart, there was a lot of swearing and an argument before he stormed out and went back to Nanna Taylor's. I don't really know what was said but I finally saw the dad that I had been waiting to come out!

We mostly spoke to dad on the phone after that for a while, which was fine with me as I still didn't know what to make of everything or how to be around dad. Tez was disappointed not to see dad, but he was only six and didn't understand the situation and he idolised his dad, whereas I saw him in a very different light. The space helped mum to work out what it was that she wanted without dad's influence. I was no longer afraid to come home or be scared about what mood dad was going to be in when he came home.

Mum never stopped us seeing dad, but he never mentioned meeting up when we spoke to him. Maybe it was because he couldn't see mum? I don't know. We had to go back to Court to finalise the custody arrangements; Dad was allowed to see us, but we were to remain living with mum full time. I was of the age to be able to speak to the Court about what I wanted, so I told them that I wanted to live with my mum. The idea of living with my dad terrified me for so many reasons!

Mum used to take Tez and I into town to meet dad and we would spend time with him for the day. Dad usually made snide remarks to Mum or to us behind her back. I continued to find it hard being around my dad and to be affectionate towards him. He had hurt us; he'd never apologised for it, and he was still being horrible to mum. I think on some level, my dad sensed this, because eventually he started being mean to me as well. I tried to ignore it, but after this behaviour I struggled to deal with any kind of personal attack on me.

A few months later, dad got a flat of his own. It wasn't too far away from Nanna Taylor, so dad was pleased. He acquired his furniture from various places, but his place lacked a homely touch as interior design clearly wasn't my dad's forte. Tez and I went over for weekends every fortnight. Dad still didn't know how to entertain two young kids, so he used to take us to see Nanna Taylor, who my brother adored and then to a pub or several. I didn't enjoy seeing Nanna Taylor. The saucepan episode always played on my mind, plus she had such an acid tongue and her manner never suggested that she regretted anything she had said or done!

Mum and dad still spoke briefly on the phone when he called to speak to us. The relationship became more civil, almost friendly at this stage during 1993 - or so I thought! The divorce had still not gone through because dad had ripped up the marriage certificate and mum had to apply for a new one with the help of Mr Bergman, her solicitor. But dad clearly wanted to talk to mum, so he invited her to his flat for dinner. Mum arranged a babysitter for us so that they could talk alone. I was immediately suspicious because although I was young, I knew my dad and I still didn't trust him with my mum.

It turns out that I was right to be wary. The morning of the day that mum was due to go to dads for dinner, her friend Val rang from down the road. I was on the other side of the room to that phone but even I heard the panic in her voice! The colour from my mum's face drained and she put the phone down. It felt confusing to me, but mum went to Val's house. I was later told that mum wasn't going to dads for dinner and the reasons why.

Dad had sent a sympathy card to Val. In it he had written *"I am sorry about the death of your friend Vonnie."* That was my mum's nickname. Mum rang dad, there was a massive argument over the phone and dad admitted what he had planned to do. He had intended to put poison in the dinner that he was going to cook! To say that I was gobsmacked was an understatement. My dad had wanted to actually kill my mum! I still get shivers thinking about this all these years later!

Mum didn't report this to the police as the legal system at the time didn't take this type of incident seriously - but maybe they would have if they had seen the card? There had been a few other 'incidents' before this too. Dad had been caught sleeping in our outside toilet which was under my bedroom window. He had arranged with various members of his local friendship circle to spy on mum when she went out and report back to him with the details of her outfit and any antics. Mum always made sure we had a babysitter; she was merely exercising her right to a social life!

Mum had a couple of boyfriends just before I hit my teenage years. The first one I quite liked despite the fact he was twenty-two years older than my mum. This made him the same age as my Nanna Brown. I don't think that she was overly impressed! He spent a lot of time at our house, so he bought his cat with him. Sadly, he cheated on mum with one of his female friends, so mum told him to collect his stuff, but the cat was staying because we had grown attached to him!

A few months later mum got involved with a local bin man. He was part of a local DJ crew who played at the local pubs on the weekends. It was a group of friends who had DJ equipment and they got paid to play some good music and socialise. As I was twelve and Tez saw dad on weekends more often than I did, I spent a few nights down at the pub with mum. There were a group of kids whose parents were out too, so I enjoyed spending some time with them.

I got on pretty well with this boyfriend as he was kind and funny. He gave me pocket money so that I could go into town with friends. But after a few months, he cheated on mum, and they broke up too. He was of course full of apologies and regrets and wanted to keep the relationship going, but mum said no as she was beginning to see her worth. She ended the relationship and fair play to her for that!

Not long after this, there was another upsetting incident with dad. We had been to see Nanna Brown and My Uncle Derek was driving us home in Nanna's car. While on a dual carriageway, a car cut between us and the car next to us and narrowly missed both cars before speeding off. We were all a little shaken and so it was decided that we would report it to the Police as the local station was in close proximity. The Police took details of the incident and the description of both cars involved, as there were also witnesses and then Derek drove us home.

We hadn't been at home too long when the phone rang, it was dad. He clearly wasn't in the best of moods and sounded like he was probably drunk. I was still upset from the car incident, so I didn't want to stay on the phone for too long with dad when he was in that state. Dad didn't take too kindly to this, so he began trying to emotionally blackmail me saying things like "you don't love your dad, you only talk to me when you want something!"

This wasn't true, mostly as there was very little I wanted from my dad by then, I spoke to him mostly because I had to, and I never asked him for anything I can assure you! This wasn't the first time that he had used these tactics, it had become a regular theme, but that day, something inside of me snapped. Instead of trying to comfort his daughter who had been in what could have been a serious accident, he was trying to emotionally blackmail me because he needed attention. I don't really remember what I actually said to dad, but I ended up going to my room in tears after handing the phone to mum.

She tried to talk to dad but also gave up and hung up on him, so mum came to check on me. I was sobbing, but I told her in no uncertain terms that I would not see or speak to dad again. Mum stood by my choice, she had seen me struggling for years with my relationship with dad after everything that had happened. I was only twelve years old, but it had all just gotten too much. This was to become a familiar theme for me when things got too difficult, and it still is, but in order to protect yourself, sometimes you just have to say no.

Chapter Two – Teenage years – not your average experiences!

After mum's previous relationship had broken up, she met up with an ex-boyfriend of a friend. This friend had a chequered history with men and this guy had apparently been hit hard by their breakup. Apparently, there was no 'girl code' preventing a woman from dating a friend's ex!

It wasn't long before he moved in. In reality, it was a little fast after the last relationship, but mum had never coped well on her own. He seemed nice, funny and he introduced us all to his parents and they seemed as lovely as he did, at least on the surface. I still wasn't talking to dad, so in some ways I was probably looking for a father figure who wasn't anything like my dad!

Reflecting upon these years, it is easy to see that he was actually grooming mum, and me, with his attentions and he made us both feel special at first. The three of us would often go on walks around the local area as Tez was at Dad's for the weekend. He would always hold my hand and there were lots of hugs and tickling. One weekend during the summer holidays, the three of us were messing about in the living room and I ended up sitting on his knee. Mum left the room and went upstairs to the toilet and the next thing I knew that he was kissing me inappropriately on the lips!

I was shocked, numb and didn't know what to do, but it happened a few more times that day when mum was out of the room.

Over the next few weeks, it kept happening and I had gone back to school by this point. It made me feel very uncomfortable. I would come home; mum would be at work, and he had me sit with him and he kissed and touched me. It felt wrong, shameful, and downright horrible, but I never struggled. I didn't know what to do or who to talk to. As time went on, he made it clear that my allowing him to touch and kiss me, would prevent him from attacking my brother and teaching him how to properly behave! I felt ashamed but somehow, I justified it because I was protecting my brother from harm.

As time evolved, his and mum's relationship changed due to what we would call his mood swings. Every month, almost like clockwork, he would have a week where he would kind of shut down. He wouldn't speak to anyone or when he did, he became aggressive. When mum tried to speak to him, it would often erupt into violence, and he would throw things, occasionally furniture. All of a sudden, this period of 'moods' would end, and he would be back to 'normal', and be attentive and apologetic towards both me and mum. I always found those periods of rejection difficult.

Although I knew what was happening was

wrong, he made me feel so special but then he wouldn't want me. It felt confusing and hurtful. I had only just turned thirteen and I didn't know how to deal with any of this. When he was in a good mood, he would pull me onto his knee, I always thought that he was going to cuddle me, and he did, but his hands went where they weren't supposed to. I always felt that there was no getting away from that shit!

The abuse and his mood swings continued, and my shame grew, and the whole situation made me more withdrawn and moodier. I think my mum put it down to teenage hormones and we'd argue, and she'd tell me that I had an attitude problem. I often thought about screaming at her and spilling out just what was going on and show her what my 'attitude problem' really was! But I never did. Her boyfriend continued to up the pressure though and he wanted me to touch him inappropriately, but I always flatly refused. He began to get annoyed with me.

When I was fourteen, the abuse was still going on as were those periods of rejection and anger. I had just started at the secondary school where I would be taking my GCSE subjects. One day I'd been listening to my Bon Jovi *'Crossroads'* cassette tape and in particular, a track called *Runaway.* After playing it on repeat all day because it summed up how I felt at the time, I decided that was it, I was going to pack my bags and leave.

I had no real plan, but I threw enough clothes for a few days into my school duffle bag. The next morning when it was time for me to leave for school, I caught the bus into town, and I walked up to the train station. I walked down towards one of the platforms with no real clue where the next train was going, and I looked at the money that I had in my small purse. I had the grand total of four pounds! Reality hit me, I couldn't afford to go anywhere, and I couldn't get caught without a ticket on a train either. If that happened, mum would have to come and get me from a police station and then I would have to tell the Police and mum that I was trying to run away. Heartbroken, and with tears in my eyes, I walked back towards Leicester City Centre and caught the bus home.

When I reached home, I knocked on the front door and no one answered. I could hear voices coming from the back garden, so I walked down towards the back gate which was unlocked. I tried to sneak through the gate and into the house via the back door, which was open before anyone saw me, but mum looked up from mowing the lawn and spotted me. There were lots of questions like "what are you doing home from school?" "What's going on?" Followed by "What's the matter with you?" because I had started to cry with panic.

I rushed up to my bedroom sobbing my heart out, frantically looking around the room trying to quickly think of a reason to give to mum. I saw my English exercise book and remembered that I hadn't done my homework, and this sparked a huge lie! Mum came in and we sat on my bed and talked. I lied and told her that I was trying to run away because I was so stressed about all my homework and that I couldn't cope with it all. I just couldn't bring myself to tell her the awful truth. I hated lying but the truth was just too dreadful to face.

Mum helped me to do my homework and she kept giving me lots of hugs the rest of the day, it was obvious that I had scared her. That really wasn't my intention, I just wanted to escape the abuse and I didn't know how to verbalise what was really going on. Things carried on as they had been, he didn't mention a thing about me trying to run away at all. I kept quiet, because I was still terrified that my abuser would carry out his threat to kill my brother. He didn't, but there were a lot of arguments and with his monthly dark moods, it often brought other problems with them.

Just before I turned fifteen, my cousin brought a friend of his to the house who was the same age as my cousin – twenty-four. Me and this friend of my cousin's had a bit of a 'thing' but nothing serious happened, but I got into trouble with mum for lying about it and because he was much too old for me! However, this gave me a break of nine months from the abuse.

My abuser couldn't look at me and he wouldn't speak to me at all. His moods got worse, but eventually though, he began to work his way back into my life. Mum had clearly noticed the atmosphere between us and encouraged me to be nicer to him, but she couldn't have known what that would mean. The horrible abuse started up again. My brother was growing up and becoming angrier with him and with mum, and so my abuser would tell me that he wanted to kill my brother unless I 'behaved.'

There were several occasions when he had applied for credit in my mum's name and spent the money. Mum was totally unaware of this until she received a letter from a credit card company informing her that her credit card had been cancelled because she owed them one thousand pounds! Mum's face went white because she hadn't applied for a credit card, but then she noticed the guilty look on his face as he skulked back to the living room. Mum stormed after him and I entered the room moments later to find mum had pinned him to the settee by the throat as she was screaming at him! Mum never reacted like this to anything, and it was quite something to see her in that state! Strangely, he didn't fight back, and his face was emotionless. I decided to leave them to discuss the situation. I was later told that he had applied for the card in mum's name and had kept watch for the envelope with the card and later the pin number to be posted through the letterbox. He had taken the card and gone onto withdraw the money from cashpoints over a period and spent the money. We never actually found out what he had spent the money on!

When I reached the age of sixteen, I left school because I wasn't happy with the A-Level subjects that I had chosen. I decided to get a job and take a year out. I began working at my local supermarket which gave me a certain amount of freedom because I had my own money. Saturday nights became a favourite. My best friend from school would often work the same shift as me at the shop.

We'd finish work at ten pm and walk home. Because we lived on the same street, we'd be in a taxi on the way to a nightclub by ten thirty. We had our going out clothes ready in our rooms before we left for work. My favourite outfit was an electric blue dress, it came to just above the knee and would often get me noticed by boys. A big smile to the right bouncer would get us through the door of the club. We had a couple of drinks each throughout the night but the majority of the time we'd be on the dance floor.

I enjoyed the attention in all honesty, but this was on my terms, no one else's. I began to have a few kisses and a couple of dates here and there. There was never anything serious. I was just a sixteen-year-old girl exploring her femininity.

Because I was getting attention and seeing boys though, I decided that the abuse was going to stop once and for all. My abuser had been making snide comments because I was no longer his and I had no intention of being his. He couldn't stand it. My brother was thirteen and had grown to just over six feet in height, almost the same height as my abuser, and it was quite clear by then that he could take care of himself if a physical situation ever arose between them.

My abuser's mental health began to decline when I put a stop to the abuse. Eventually he saw a doctor and later a psychiatrist, who diagnosed manic depression which, later became known as bipolar disorder. He was prescribed medication and occasionally he threatened to or tried to overdose on them. I saw mum wrestling to obtain the packet of medication from his hands at least once. Tez lived with dad for a while, but unfortunately, dad wasn't particularly good at sending him to school, so we had to bring him home. Dad's mental health declined too. Tez had been on a holiday to Skegness with him and dad had sworn that the caravan had been picked up and turned around in the opposite direction! Poor Tez didn't know what to do with him, he was way too young. He coped in the best way that he could.

There was a period where mum, my abuser and I were all working in the same shoe warehouse. I had worked there previously during the summer before my GCSE results, so I knew the company well. Within a week, I was asked to work in the office, leaving him and mum in the warehouse. He was head warehouseman, and part of that role was to report the weekly in/out delivery figures to me. During one of his bad periods, he refused to speak to me and mum, and the supervisor of the company wanted those weekly figures from me. I had to tell her that he wouldn't give them to me. She went out to the warehouse to speak to him, and she had no joy from him either. She asked mum to go and try, again he refused to speak to mum.

He ended up throwing his gloves across the warehouse in a huge rage and shouting obscenities before quitting his job. He rarely held down a job for long; he was too unstable. Mum and I were called into the company owner's office after he heard about the debacle from the supervisor, and he wanted to know what had just happened. Mum was crying as she explained about him, his 'moods' and the debts. We were both terrified that we were going to be fired over the incident. We had generally managed to keep a lid on how he was at home, and I still kept my secret close to my chest. The boss told the supervisor to get the vital figures from someone else and sent us both back to work. Being at work was the best thing for us both as neither of us wanted to go home to deal with him in his current state.

Chapter Three - The headiness of first love!

When I was seventeen years old, I returned to the supermarket where I had worked whilst I was at college. My friend still worked there, and she was dating a local lad who also worked with us. He invited us both round to his house on New Year's Eve for a film night with pizza and we were asked to bring some drinks. It never occurred to me to refuse the invitation because I'd be the third wheel! We watched the latest James Bond film that had been released onto video. There was also some music, a little bit of drinking and a lot of laughter! His parents had recently had dial-up internet installed (who remembers that noise?) Their service provider had various online chatrooms, so he showed us some of them and how to access them.

Somehow, I ended up chatting to a guy in Worcester. We swapped numbers pretty quickly and we ended up chatting on our mobiles for a little while. I think I experienced a little Dutch courage from whatever it was that I had been drinking that night! He was a couple of years older than me, seemed nice and he promised to call me the next day. I hung up feeling cheerful and a little merry, but slightly cynical. I didn't believe that he would call me.

He actually did call me; I was utterly

amazed! He told me that he was two years older than me. He had a car, and he had his own house in Worcester. We continued to chat over the coming days. Mum was happy for me but of course my abuser had gone into another huge sulk because I was having contact with another male, but I didn't care. Eventually my admirer and I arranged our first date, he agreed to drive to Leicester as it was easier. We arranged to meet at the Clock Tower (I told you it was THE meeting place in Leicester, it is well sign posted!). It was a Sunday, so it was pretty quiet, and we decided to go to the cinema. *Enemy of the State* had just been released and so off we went.

We both enjoyed the film and afterwards we walked around the city centre for a while, but with little to do, I asked him if he would like to come back to my house and meet my mum! He actually agreed - you can probably gather that I was not used to dating boys and I didn't want him to drive home yet. This was the only way I could think of to spend a bit more time with him as I was technically underage to drink, and as he was driving, pubs were out of the question anyway.

We arrived at my house and mum was very welcoming and made us all a cup of tea. We all chatted in the living room. I liked him. Mum seemed to like him too and he seemed quite relaxed chatting with my mum. After a couple of hours, he told me that he needed to drive back to Worcester as he had to work the following morning and he didn't want to be too tired.

I walked him out of the house and towards his car. I turned to kiss him on the cheek but before I knew what was happening, he pulled me towards him and gave me a full-on kiss on the lips. I enjoyed that kiss and it felt right and real, so I reciprocated. I walked back into the house with a goofy smile on my face floating on a cloud. Mum saw the smile and asked when I would be seeing him again. I told her that he was coming back in a couple of days after he finished work. Knowing that she liked him made me happy.

The next day at college, I saw my best friend and told her all about my date. I wanted her to meet him so I asked her to come round to my house the following evening so they could be introduced. The next day at college absolutely dragged and I couldn't concentrate - I don't mind admitting it! I rushed home and told my friend to come round to mine for about seven that evening. Mum could sense my anticipation and told me not to rush my dinner.

My friend arrived about twenty minutes before he did. When he arrived, we all sat upstairs in my bedroom. I had a sofa-bed that I had converted into a sofa, so we all had room to sit down and chat. I left the bedroom door ajar to appease mum as I had a boy in my room. My friend told us that she was leaving us after about an hour, she told me there was no need for me to see her out with a knowing look. As soon as she had left the room, we pounced on each other! We kissed a lot that evening, but I wanted to take things slow, so we talked and found out more about each other.

Over the next few weeks, he drove down to Leicester to see me at least twice a week. We went to the cinema and spent time at my house. Things went well and although we didn't have a lot in common, there was a spark between us that couldn't be ignored. We came from different backgrounds, and he had a maturity that I appreciated. I had never really been interested in boys at school or college. Valentine's Day was coming up so I asked mum if he could come and stay with us for the weekend. Mum said no as she was trying to protect me, but it didn't matter as when I spoke to him about it, he invited me over to his for the weekend instead. I was over the moon just to be spending time away from home as there was an unpleasant tension I felt from my abuser because I was dating someone. I was happy and while mum had her reservations, she didn't stop me from going to Worcester.

I had to get two trains. I didn't have a lot of experience travelling alone but I had been given instructions and train times, so I made it to Worcester safely via Birmingham. He was waiting on the train platform for me when I arrived and took my bag from me as he gave me a kiss on the lips. He took my hand and took me down to where he had parked his car.

I wasn't sure what to make of Worcester as a place as he drove us to his house, but I did have butterflies in my tummy. He parked outside a row of houses, the middle one turned out to be his. He opened the front door, and a black and white cat, Minstrel, came to greet us. He was unsure of me at first and it took a long time for him to get used to me!

I was cooked a meal and then we sat on the sofa watching television and talking. Later that evening, he poured us both some wine. I sipped it slowly, still feeling the butterflies dancing in my stomach. I began to feel more nervous, and he could tell as he pulled me to him. He kissed me and assured me that nothing was expected of me if I didn't want to do anything yet. I breathed a sigh of relief, and he took my hand and led me upstairs. We both changed and took turns in the bathroom. It was a one-bedroom house, so we were going to be sharing a bed if nothing else. This was a first for me. He pulled me into a hug, and we didn't really sleep that night. I couldn't settle, so we talked, kissed, and cuddled pretty much all night. He was a total gentleman, to his credit.

The next morning, we both showered and dressed and decided to head into Birmingham as it was only a forty-minute drive. We had chatted about going to Birmingham during the last few weeks and I was keen to go. I was still a little anxious and what I call antsy. I fell in love with Birmingham, it was bigger than Leicester and different, so it felt exciting. It is still one of my favourite places to this day! He took me for a late lunch at a café in the Convention Centre. I struggled to eat any of it - my nervousness had begun to affect my appetite! He squeezed my hand as he led me back to the car to drive us back to Worcester. I was still a little excitable on the way back, with lots of laughter and singing in the car!

We arrived back and as it was only late afternoon and neither of us had slept much the night before, we decided to have a nap. I did settle eventually, and I woke up hungry! He cooked us dinner again and we checked out his local paper for cinema times for the Worcester Odeon. We discovered that *This Year's Love* was playing. We had watched the trailer the evening before and so we decided to go and watch it and drove into Worcester City Centre. It felt really small compared to both Leicester and Birmingham. We both enjoyed the film and by then, I was feeling giddy with excitement as I had made a decision. I wanted to lose my virginity that night! We walked along holding hands and giggling and I pushed him against a wall to kiss him. I whispered my intentions for that night and bit his earlobe. We reached the car and he drove us back to his house. I felt more settled in myself. He poured us both some wine and we settled ourselves on the sofa. I think that we were both a little nervous. We kissed and chatted and out of the corner of my eye, I noticed Minstrel trying to get at my full glass of wine. I instinctively grabbed the glass and drank all my wine at once!

As the evening wore on, we both began to yawn, and we decided to go to bed. My nerves began to kick back in, and the wine had gone to my head a little. To cut a long story short, I passed out in bed at exactly the wrong moment scaring him half to death! I came to, immediately aware that I was stark naked, feeling woozy and he was shaking my arm vigorously. I reassured him that I was awake and asked him what happened.

He told me what had happened; things between us had not progressed as far as we had originally intended. I was somewhat grateful. I don't know if it had been the wine or whether it was an anxiety reaction, to prevent the physical act that I was not yet ready for. I cuddled into him, and we talked for a while about everything but what had happened and why. I avoided the subject, and he didn't want to press the situation thankfully. I fell into a deep sleep as I had not slept very much since I had arrived on Friday!

The next morning, we had a leisurely breakfast and we drove into the centre of Worcester as I was getting the train back to Birmingham later on. We walked around Worcester, it still seemed small even in the daylight, but it had a quaintness about it. We ate a late lunch at a fast-food place before he walked me to the train station. I was sorry to be leaving, it felt like we had been in a little bubble, and I was returning to a reality that I was not happy in. I couldn't tell him about the abuse. He knew a little about my dad, but I just could not bring myself to confess that I had been sexually abused by my mother's boyfriend and that was possibly the reason why I had been unable to lose my virginity the night before.

I caught the train back into Birmingham, feeling incredibly sad to be leaving him and to be going home. Despite my passing out the night before, I had enjoyed the weekend, I only hoped that we would continue to see each other and that I hadn't scared him off! I needn't have worried, he called me that evening when I got home to check I had arrived safely.

I assured him that I had and that I was fine. I didn't stay on the phone for too long because I was holding back my tears and I didn't want him to hear the crack in my voice. Mum had been pleased to see me, but we didn't talk much about what happened, I wasn't ready for that conversation. I did tell her about the wine and the passing out though, but I made a huge joke of it, so she laughed.

We did continue to see each other regularly over the coming weeks and months and I visited his place often. I didn't feel comfortable with him staying at mine, so I never asked mum again and he had his cat to feed anyway. I did use his place as my bolthole when things weren't going well though and I began to get in trouble with my college because of this. I had one particularly traumatic exam for Business Studies, and I knew that I hadn't done too well. I went to the office and feigned a migraine, so they let me go home after the exam. I went home and left a note for my mum, packed a bag, and left for Worcester. It was only Tuesday; I hadn't been scheduled for work that weekend and it was a bank holiday weekend too so I worked out that I would have nearly a week in Worcester! He had asked me to go over for the weekend anyway, so I was just arriving a few days early. It was still his lunchtime, so a quick call whilst I was whizzing around the house packing my bag confirmed that he was more than happy for me to go and stay but he would be working until Friday evening. This didn't bother me as long as I wasn't at home!

We had a lovely week together. But when he brought me home on the Tuesday evening, mum came into the bedroom with a stern look on her face. The college had written to her because I had taken more time off than they would normally expect for illness. I had missed college that day too as I should have come home the day before. Admittedly, some of it had been illness, but I had developed a nasty habit of leaving early on a Friday to avoid the evening rush on the trains to Worcester.

However, we both made a promise that I would make more of an effort to attend college regularly and stop the early finishes on a Friday. I did keep my promise and I attended college as I should for the rest of that academic year. But it became apparent with the more exams I took just how much I was not enjoying my courses, and none of it came naturally to me which I was not used to at all. I realised that if my heart was not in it, there was very little point in me continuing. Things between me and my boyfriend were serious, and I never had a life plan anyway. had also gotten used to having money in my pocket whilst I was working for that year. About two weeks before the end of the year, my exams had finished, and I had nothing to do, so I went to the office and completed the form to finish my studies at college.

I don't think that I had told mum of my intentions, but she may have had some idea of where things were going. My boyfriend had asked me to move in for the summer to see how I liked being in Worcester. I did look for jobs in Worcester, but sadly I didn't get anything for the summer, so I spent my weekdays in Worcester and came home for the weekends to work at the supermarket or the other way around depending on how my rota was organised.

It took a few months of interviews and registering with agencies before I actually secured an office role. By this time, it was November and having spoken to them on Thursday, they wanted me to start the role on the following Monday! I was over the moon, but I had to call the supermarket and tell them that I was quitting without giving notice because I had no choice. The supervisor was less than thrilled but she rarely got excited about anything!

I then had to tell my mum that we would be driving over at the weekend to collect the rest of my things because I was moving in with my boyfriend. Mum was pleased for me as she knew that I had been looking for a job for a while. I was relieved that the backwards and forwards travelling between Leicester and Worcester would be over. I had found travelling quite tiring. I was excited and daunted in equal measure, as I was only eighteen years old, and I was leaving home permanently! Mum had pretty much done the same thing at my age, but she remained in Leicester, I was leaving my hometown for somewhere that I was still slightly unsure of. But I was in love, and we wanted to be together.

That weekend, we drove over to mums to collect the rest of my belongings. It felt strange knowing that I wouldn't be sleeping in my room again - I had a feeling that my brother was set to claim it just as soon as I was out of the door! Mum helped me to pack everything up. We were both a little tearful, but as my abuser was in the house and I still had not plucked up the courage to talk to mum about it, I could not wait to leave! He actually refused to speak to me or my boyfriend for the whole time that we were there that day. Mum couldn't understand why, and I just brushed it off.

She suggested that the three of us go for a drink before we loaded the car up to leave. We went to a local pub, and we only stayed for about an hour. I was feeling a little nervous as part of me wanted to tell mum the truth and then run away. In all honesty, I could never have done that to her. Having seen how she reacted over the credit card, I was fairly sure that she would end up being arrested for grievous bodily harm or murder and I would have to come back home. Just keeping quiet felt like my only option and this became a pattern for many years to come!

We left my mums house with my boyfriend's fiesta full to the brim with my stuff packed away in bags and boxes. We were both happy and giddy on the way home – my new home. The task of unpacking wasn't as bad as it could have been as he had cleared room for my stuff including a whole wardrobe for my clothes, I was impressed! Admittedly, that wardrobe was a little too small and it wobbled, but my clothes were put away. We both went to bed that evening tired but happy. The following morning was to be day one at my new job.

My first day was a whirlwind - new people to meet and many new things to get my head around. I reached home at the end of the day exhausted, and it really caught up with me a little later that evening. We had just finished dinner, when a black cloud came over me and I began to sob uncontrollably. My poor boyfriend didn't know what to make of the situation, but I could only put it down to the fact that it was due to the changes in my life that had taken place.

I wasn't unhappy, far from it, but I was away from home, I didn't have any friends in the neighbourhood and as far as I was concerned, going home was absolutely not an option! He consoled me until I calmed down and we talked, and he reassured me that we could load up the car and he would take me back to mum's if that is what I wanted. I told him that it wasn't, it was just the impact of all of the changes getting the better of me.

My mood did settle down over the coming days. It was December and there was still Christmas to think about. My boyfriend was going back to his parents, so it was clear that I was going back to mums for a few days. Somehow, mum had managed to prevent my brother from claiming my bedroom just yet! We drove over on Christmas day morning. His parents lived in Ipswich, so he was able to drop me off in Leicester on the way. Christmas was lovely but strange. My abuser's mood had settled in time for the day to be pleasant thankfully, but I ensured that I kept my distance and kept any conversations light. My boyfriend and I wanted to celebrate New Year together, so he collected me two or three days after Christmas. His parents were curious about why he was so definite about going home but he hadn't told them the full story about our relationship. That was to become one of his regular patterns!

Over the coming months, we both settled into our daily routines of going to work and coming home. We both had work colleagues but no real friends outside of work, so we only really had each other. It didn't really feel strange to either of us. I still kept in contact with my friends from Leicester via text and phone calls, but my best friend had gone to University in Preston. My boyfriend went back to his parent's house for the odd weekend, and I stayed at home in Worcester. Those weekends felt a little lonely and I tried to keep myself occupied as best I could.

It became apparent that his parents knew nothing about our relationship. He had a phone that displayed the caller identification. When the landline rang and his parent's number came up, he wouldn't let me answer the phone and he told me that I had to be quiet whilst he was on the phone to them! I tried to talk to him about it, but he would just shut me down and say that they wouldn't understand. My relationship with my mum was really good so I was confused by his reply, but I chose not to press him too much.

Unfortunately, it seemed that I had a habit of getting ill which meant taking time off work. The final straw came which was after we had been cycling in the New Forest for a weekend away. On the Monday morning, I woke up with really severe cramps in my legs and could not get out of bed, let alone get to work. I went to the doctor's the next morning prior to going to work. The doctor could not find anything wrong with me as usual. I had been to see them a few times with varying symptoms such as migraines, muscular cramps and pains and low energy levels. Various medications and vitamins had been prescribed but nothing seemed to work. I went into work after my appointment and my boss called me into his office.

He sat me down and told me that the company were struggling financially. I knew this to be true as I was the Sales Administrator, and it was clear that we had not made enough sales over the last few months. As I was the last person to be hired, I would be the first person to be let go, and with my sickness history he couldn't find a reason to fight to keep me on. He asked if I wanted to work the rest of the day or leave there and then, so I told him that I would like to leave straightaway.

I felt upset, and I knew I would struggle to

keep my emotions in check for the rest of the day. I called my boyfriend on the way home to let him know what the doctor had said and the situation with my job. I was worried sick that he would send me packing back home if I didn't have a job and I couldn't afford to pay my way. Luckily, he was pretty sweet about it, and he reassured me that I just needed to find another job. Nevertheless, I went to bed and had a damn good cry once I arrived home!

It didn't take long before I found another job and fortunately, the salary was higher than the last one. I liked my new workplace, the team I worked with were great and there were many laughs throughout the day! With my higher salary, we were able to afford a holiday abroad in the July of that year. We booked two weeks in Zakynthos, one of the Greek islands. This was my first time on a plane, and I was excited and nervous all at the same time.

The holiday was amazing, the island was beautiful, and I fully relaxed for the first time in a really long time. I felt the weight drop from my shoulders; I hadn't experienced that feeling before. However, the holiday wasn't entirely without incident. My mum and my brother had popped over to our house in Worcester to check on Minstrel, the cat. He was being fed by our neighbours whilst we were away. When we called mum over the weekend, she had to break the news that Minstrel had gone missing. She had popped out to do some shopping and when she returned to the house, there were two different chunks of fur in the kitchen along with a few blood splatters.

It was clear that there had been a cat fight. The cat flap was open to enable Minstrel to come and go as he pleased as he didn't appreciate being locked in the house. My boyfriend's mood changed after hearing this news. We were too far away to actually do much about it and then two days after we had been unable to reach mum, there was more news that wasn't cat related. My brother, Tez had been admitted to hospital with appendicitis. Luckily, his appendix had held out until he had reached the hospital but if he had been travelling back to Leicester on the train as planned, he would have died apparently! His appendix had to be removed and he spent three days in hospital recovering. My concern was for my brother because I couldn't do anything. My boyfriend on the other hand could only care for his cat. There was not one iota of care for my brother. This made me angry and we had words a couple of times about his attitude.

Things were further hampered when we attended a Greek night up in the mountains on the island. There were a lot of trees overhanging the area where we were eating and dancing. As we were walking back towards the coach, I felt something land on my arm. It was the biggest spider that I had ever seen in my life to that point. I am terrified of spiders; I always have been and probably always will be. I let out a scream and most of the attendees jumped and turned to see what the racket was. I brushed the spider off as I screamed and I started to cry and, on some level, I went into shock. I shut down and became mute and continued to cry on the coach back to the hotel. My boyfriend's reaction was not one of care, but more one of embarrassment with my screams and crying.

We reached our resort and he guided me to a bar where we had previously enjoyed some cocktails. He went to the bar and came back with several of my favourite cocktails. I couldn't decide if he was trying to help with the shock or sweeten me up, but I drank them anyway. I continued not to talk to him once the alcohol was in my system and I was over the shock. A short while later, he decided to force the issue. According to him, I had overreacted about the spider and my brother was perfectly fine so I needed to grow up. I got angry with him, and he offered no apology and didn't take my feelings into account. I probably had drunk a few too many cocktails by that point so I stormed off and left him sitting in the bar! I found my way back to our hotel via the beach and I sat in our room and had a good cry. I was drunk and angry - rarely a good combination for me.

He arrived a short while later, he was also

drunk but he was still angry with me. My heart began to beat faster in response. The only drunk angry man that I had encountered in my life was my dad and I was worried that I was about to get a pasting and so I backed towards the back of the room. I needn't have worried, he apologised for arguing with me and for making me feel that he didn't care about me, and he had tears in his eyes. I am a sucker for anyone who cries at me, so I did what I normally do, I hugged him and kissed him. I apologised for storming off and worrying him and all was well in our relationship again, at least for a time!

Two days after returning from our holiday, the cat returned home. I wasn't entirely thrilled in all honesty as he scratched me a lot and I considered him to be a mean cat. We returned to work and our routines had not changed much, until one particular Friday a few months later.

I was getting my lunch ready for work whilst my boyfriend was upstairs getting ready, and I accidently knocked his paper driving license off the kitchen worktop onto the floor. My curiosity was piqued as I bent down to pick it up. I did have a provisional license of my own so I knew that his license would look slightly different from mine, but I opened it up to see the dates that his license was valid from and to. I was expecting to see similar dates to mine as he was only two years older than me. But the dates were vastly different by about ten years, so I checked the date of birth on the license as that had to be an error and I could tell him to get in touch with DVLA to get it corrected.

His date of birth wasn't what I had been led to believe. He wasn't two years older than me; he was actually ten years older than me! I felt like a fool, and I was shocked and livid that I had been lied to. But as we both had work to go to that day, I chose to keep quiet until we got home later. I had the whole day to ruminate on this new information about my boyfriend and his lie. I couldn't concentrate and it was being noticed at work, so I tried to put it down to tiredness. I didn't wait for my boyfriend to finish work and collect me in our usual meeting place that day, I went straight home on the bus. I felt exhausted, trying to keep everything in all day had clearly taken an effect on me and so I tried to rest until he came home.

I awoke when I heard my boyfriend come through the front door. I was like a woman possessed, I had been thinking about his lie all damn day and now I was going to get some answers! I flew down the stairs like a mad woman and he was shocked by my demeanour as he immediately asked what was wrong with me. I grabbed his driving license off the side and threw it at him, demanding to know what his real age was. He didn't even try to lie his way out of it, it was quite clear from the way that I was acting that it would be a waste of time. We argued because I felt so damn betrayed! I had been carrying his passport in my handbag whilst we were on holiday, and not once had I noticed that his date of birth was different. I had even bought him a birthday card to celebrate his '21st' birthday earlier in the year. At least now it made sense why his parents hadn't done the same or made a big fuss out of it, because he was actually twenty-nine!

I was fed up with the arguing as we kept going round in circles; he was sorry, and I was angry that he had lied to me. I went upstairs and locked myself in the bathroom for a while whilst I had a bloody good cry. I had decided that going home to mum's wasn't an option for me. I went back downstairs, and we talked. I agreed to stay, and he agreed that there would be no more lies.

Things went back to normal, as though the lie had never happened and a part of me began to revel in having a relationship with an older man! But things were different between us, at least to me, and it felt a little more strained. I couldn't tell my mum that he was older than me as she would have insisted that if he had lied about that, he could lie again and that I should come home. My mother had clearly never taken her own advice here! It was a few months down the line and my boyfriend had finally told his parents that he was in a relationship. We even visited them for a weekend before we had a short break on the Norfolk Broads, but he still had not told them that we were living together.

I was struck by ill health one week and I didn't know what was wrong. I strongly suspect it was an early period of depression. I was depleted of energy, physically and mentally. We had been bickering for a while beforehand. I didn't go to work all week and I knew that I could self-certify for a week without visiting the doctors for a sick note. By the end of that week, I had begun to feel better so my boyfriend decided that he would go to visit his parents for the weekend as planned and that I could spend the weekend recuperating at home. I felt a little bit put out, but a part of me wanted the house to myself.

As usual, he left me a list of things that could be done around the house, I think he was forgetting that I had been ill all that week. He called regularly throughout the weekend, but he wasn't concerned about my welfare, instead, he was checking to see if I had done any of the chores that he had left for me. I resented those calls. I was still feeling out of sorts, and he didn't once ask me how I was feeling. By the time he returned home on Sunday evening, I was livid. As soon as he got in the door, we argued, and I snapped. I told him that our relationship was over and that I wanted to leave.

I stormed out of the house, and I went for

a walk as I wanted to call my mum in peace. She told me that she would call my Uncle Derek and ask him to come and collect me if I was ready to pack my things. I told her that, I was sure. I wasn't and I didn't know what I was returning to back at mums, but I knew that I couldn't cope with my relationship anymore. I also knew that I couldn't afford to get a place of my own in Worcester and it wasn't somewhere that I wanted to stay and make my home. I returned to the house; my boyfriend had put the bolt across so I couldn't get in with my key. I knocked the door, and he opened it. As soon as he saw that it was me, he tried to close it again, but I was quick to put my foot in the door and barged it open.

I told him that I was leaving as my phone rang. It was mum confirming that my uncle was coming to get me that night. I ran upstairs and pulled my suitcases off the top of the wardrobe. I threw all my things into the cases, and I had to virtually sit on them to get them to zip up. I put some leftover items into black bin bags as I had accrued more belongings since I had left mum's house! We bickered the entire time that we were waiting for my mum and my uncle to arrive. He did try to apologise at one point but after some of the awful things that he had called me and my family, I was in no mood to listen or take on the apology!

Mum and Derek arrived, and while we loaded up his car, my boyfriend didn't utter a word to either of them. Mum did try to talk to him, but he simply ignored her. The car was full, and we were about to pull away and the worst possible thing happened. My Uncle's car refused to start! I had to knock on my now ex-boyfriend's door and ask if he had any jump leads. He didn't have any and he shut the door in my face. We had to call out the AA to help us. I was so embarrassed as we had to wait in the car outside my ex-boyfriend's house with a car full of my belongings! Mum could sense my need to just get back home to her house and away from this situation, so she hugged me close whilst we waited for the breakdown company. They told my uncle that his alternator was broken and that he would need a new one, but they gave us a jump start so we could get back to Leicester. We arrived back at mum's at about 1.30am, she and my uncle unloaded the car and left my belongings in her living room. Luckily, mum had my bed ready so I could just go on up and get straight in. We were all exhausted, I promised to call my uncle the day after, and he drove home. He still had to go to work in the morning whilst, mum and I would be able to have a lie in.

Chapter Four – Being Back Home

Mum woke me with a cup of tea the next morning. I realised that I still needed to call work as they would be wondering where I was. My supervisor was very kind and understanding once I had told her that I was back in Leicester. She told me that she would sort out the paperwork if I sent her a resignation letter which I was happy to do.

Mum and I chatted over breakfast; she was a little surprised that I had called off the relationship. We talked and I think she understood when I told her about his parents not knowing that we were even living together. For some reason, I held back on telling her about his real age and his lying to me. I still don't know why, but it was several years before I could bring myself to admit to that too. I asked mum if her partner was around, but he was at work. I was relieved, I needed a little more time before I could face him again. I was amazed that my abuser had secured a job, but mum told me that he had been there for a couple of months by this point, and she was hopeful that he would remain there for a while. I didn't hold my breath based on his history! His 'moods' meant that he didn't hold down a job for very long, because there was always something wrong with the job or his bosses were 'against him.'

He returned from work later that evening after mum and I had spent the day unpacking my things back into my old room. He was in a relatively good mood which I was relieved about. There was a sense that we were 'dancing around each other' a bit. We had barely been in the same room together, let alone the same household, in the eighteen months that I had been in Worcester. Luckily, over the coming days, things at mum's settled down. There appeared to be an unspoken agreement between me and my abuser to just get on with things. So, we did, we kept things mostly civil, and I kept him at arm's length or more trust me!

I began job hunting and I registered with a local employment agency. They placed me with an insurance company which was close to mum's house, providing their data entry. I wasn't yet ready to consider it as home and it felt strange to be back living there.

Meanwhile, I had started speaking again to my ex on the phone, after he had said some lovely words and gradually, we were kind of making a go of things long distance. I had no intention of moving back in with him and I had made that clear. I spent a weekend with him, and it was weird. He came to collect me from mums, and he was quite sarcastic with her and there was no need for it at all! I returned to mums on the Sunday evening, and I was fairly sure that I was definitely going to end things permanently.

We spoke during that week, and he virtually demanded that I go back to Worcester that weekend! I had already made plans with the family to visit the Zoo. We hadn't really had much proper family time since I had returned to Leicester, and I was looking forward to it. He wasn't pleased when I told him this and so we argued, particularly when he began to call my mum and my brother horrible names. It was the final straw for me, this was not someone that I wanted to be with. I made it clear that things between us were definitely over and I hung up on him. I will admit that it wasn't my most mature move, but it gave me some satisfaction at the time! Mum had heard the conversation and so came to comfort me. She had known that I was feeling a bit 'off' about our relationship since moving back and now she understood something in me had 'snapped' for want of a better word.

I carried on as usual for a few days, I didn't want to or feel the need to mope. I was glad to have drawn a line under things. My mind was very compartmentalised back then. My brain had lots of little boxes, and this one was now closed and filed away. One morning, a few days after that phone call, I received a very neatly written envelope. I recognised the handwriting immediately as my ex-boyfriend's and the post mark was Worcester. The letter was full of the usual apologies and romantic notions that were not getting past the stone wall that I had now erected.

He did talk about the fact that we had never connected properly physically since the night that I had passed out during that first weekend. I had never been able to be honest with him about my sexual abuse and I wasn't about to be now! We had done some things, but we had never gone the whole way. I was too nervous about it and just couldn't, and he had never pushed things, and neither of us tried to talk about things openly. I realised that this was a sign our relationship wasn't particularly healthy if we couldn't even communicate about sex or the lack of it! He still hadn't even asked why in his letter.

I considered writing back, but I decided that it wouldn't change anything, so I threw his letter away. A few days later, roses were delivered to the house with a teddy bear! There was a card with more romantic notions. Again, these washed over me. I decided to call him to ask him to please stop and tell him that things were not going to change from my perspective! He was angry and began ranting at me, very different from all the platitudes and drivel written in the letter and the card! Anyone who knows me will know that the last thing you should do is rant at me! I shouted back at him to leave me alone and hung up on him again.

My next move was to drive the point home a little more, so I took the heads off the roses and cut up the card and the letter and put them in the envelope with both mine and mum's keys to his house with a note to leave me alone in big capital letters. Mum posted it for me the next morning and that was the last that I ever heard from him!

I do sometimes wonder what he is doing now, more than twenty years later. Part of me would like to tell him the truth about my abuse but, in all honesty, it doesn't change anything. I don't think that we could ever be friends and I wouldn't want to now. I was too young and naïve, and he had lied and didn't know how to communicate about difficult things. Our relationship really had been doomed - hindsight really is wonderful, isn't it?

I was relieved that the drama was over and so I just carried on as normal. This was becoming a pattern; my abuser was still in the house and showed no signs of going anywhere and mum didn't seem to have any intentions of getting rid of him either. We remained civil but every now and then, he would comment on something. I only had to throw him a look or make a remark and he instantly stopped. I had no intention of saying anything to mum at this point, as I was beginning to enjoy my new feeling of power - I won't lie! We continued this way for quite some time to mum's bemusement. I don't think she had any real sense of what was going on between us. She knew that neither of us liked the other.

In time though, my abusers 'moods' began to play a bigger part again. He quit his latest job and arguments began between him and mum again. He refused to talk and throwing things around was his choice of communication. He was prescribed more medication. Sadly, this didn't seem to help him at all and one day he threatened to overdose. This resulted in both mum and I wrestling to take away his pills from him. There was no real knowledge or sharing of mental health back then, but to be fair, I didn't have any particular sympathy for him either.

By the time I was twenty, mum began carving a bit more of a life for herself outside of the house. She was socialising with friends. I had a computer and the broadband had been installed so you could use the phone and the internet at the same time. Mum had seen me use a few chatrooms when I was bored so she asked me to show her how to use them. Mum had never really used computers before, so we started with the basics, such as how to turn the machine on. She wrote all the steps down on a pad and I got her registered on one or two chatrooms. Mum seemed to be enjoying herself chatting online. I told her that if she wanted to use the computer whilst I was out, she could. Apparently, she did. She told me that she had been chatting to a lorry driver from

Portsmouth. She said that he was nice and that they were getting on.

There was a glint in her eye again and she was acting in a giddy manner! Meanwhile, her partner was being more difficult than ever. Mum seemed to be finding a source of strength because she was taking a lot less of it on board than before. It wasn't long until there was a major argument.

Mum told him that she couldn't take anymore and that she wanted him to move out. He ended up moving into his parent's house in the village centre. He asked if he could take the dining table and chairs that he had paid for. Mum said yes, but apparently before his dad came to collect them, she took all the loose screws and 'mislaid' the bag containing them!

The relief at him moving out was immense, it really was! Life settled down, mostly. Tez was still experiencing dramatic episodes with our dad, but I couldn't deal with that at this point. I just needed things to settle down for a while. Mum was spending more time online chatting with the truck driver from Portsmouth. If she wasn't online or at work, she was out with a gay couple that she knew from work. They were good fun to be around. Eventually, mum received a message that her truck driver would be in Leicester overnight on his delivery route. Mum was like a giggling schoolgirl honestly!

They met up where he parked the lorry and

then they came back to the house. He had dinner with us all. He seemed like a nice bloke, but I was worried that it was too soon for mum to be getting involved with someone else so quickly. I wasn't feeling too well as I had been struggling to sleep so I took a sleeping tablet and went to bed. The next morning, I came downstairs, and the truck driver was still there, he had clearly spent the night! Part of me was shocked and there was another part of me that really wasn't. I know my mum and I love her dearly, but she doesn't function well alone, despite her protestations to this point!

He went back to his lorry and on towards Portsmouth and mum returned home still in a good mood. She called her friends over. I don't remember if they expressed their concerns at this point or not. I was not ready to give this relationship any kind of blessing. I began to spend more time with mum's friends than she did. I got quite close to one of them, we had similar personalities, so we had some major laughs. His husband was lovely, but he was the 'father figure' to us, the naughty school children, he was always telling us off for something!

Mum's truck driver came to Leicester a few more times and I began to get angrier with mum. Why couldn't she just let us all recover from her last relationship for a while before bringing another man into the house? The more often he visited, the more I would spend time with my gay

DEALING WITH IT

friends because they disapproved and hated him as much as I did!

Tez and I were having a joint birthday party in the September of that year. I was turning twenty-one and Tez would be eighteen. Mum hired the hall at a local pub, and we invited friends and family. It was a great night. Mum invited her truck driver to the party, and he stayed with us for a couple of days. Mum sat my brother and I down shortly before he left. She told us that he would be moving in with us in a couple of weeks. I didn't feel like we knew him well enough to be living with him just yet and I didn't really think that mum did either! Here she was leaping without thinking again, at least that is how I felt!

He moved in, he seemed like a nice guy, but I wasn't ready to give him an easy ride just yet. I went to work and then onto my friend's house regularly and came home not long before bedtime. I was full of anger, resentment, and a certain level of hate too. My friends asked me to join them on holiday to Florida that November. I was so excited! I needed more money, so I left the job that I was doing and began working for a local bank's administration centre.

I had to travel alone from Gatwick to Florida via New Jersey. My friends saw me off before catching their direct flight. I was nervous about travelling alone but I made it. Florida was amazing! We visited the Disney Parks and

69

Universal Studios. I did too much shopping, I remember that! I loved being in America. For a laugh, the three of us decided to take a look at an apartment in a gated complex. It was a two-bedroom place, both of which were ensuite and had walk in closets. There were tennis courts, a laundry, and communal gardens on the complex. I was smitten and the rental price in America was so much cheaper than in the UK.

The three of us did sit down and discuss the idea of moving to America together but we were also aware that America's immigration system would make it damn near impossible! But the two of them were putting their house back on the market and they asked me how I felt about moving in with them when they found a new house. Of course, I said yes, and we made plans to house hunt together on our return to the UK. I was desperate to move out of mum's and get some space from her new relationship. I'd had enough and they understood.

We returned to the wintry weather in the UK, a shock to the system having been walking around in T-shirts and shorts in December back in America! I had only been home for a couple of days when the guys called–- they were viewing a four bedroomed house in a newly built area of Leicester. I went with them, and we all loved the house, there was so much space, and I knew exactly which room I wanted!

Mum was beginning to get concerned about how much time I was spending with the guys. I didn't do much to allay her fears when I told her that I was moving out when they had secured their new house because I didn't want to be at home anymore! I told mum what they were saying about her new relationship, and that I felt the same and that's why I spent so much time with them. She wasn't surprised but mum had that look on her face that told me she wasn't happy! I was, and still can be incredibly headstrong and I was angry with mum!

We were getting closer to Christmas, so I began to spend a bit more time at home, although begrudgingly. The guys were busy and had stuff to do with the house too. Slowly, I began to see mum's boyfriend in a new light. He was essentially a good bloke, and he cared a lot for mum, that much was obvious. He was nothing like her last partner and I realised that maybe I should give him a chance. He and I got on well, it took me a while to understand his dry sense of humour admittedly. We developed a sense of banter between us, and mum got in on it too sometimes. My brother was spending a lot of time with dad as usual and he was quiet so, we generally let him be for the sake of peace.

Christmas came and it was a lovely day and mum's partner bought her some lovely presents and treated her like a queen. This stopped me in my tracks, and I realised then and there, that I didn't want to move in with the guys anymore. I knew that if I did, I would lose my mum, and for all her faults, that wasn't something that I was willing to do. She just didn't know how to live by herself, and this man loved her and treated her like a queen, and he didn't treat me and my brother badly or try to abuse me! So much of my anger had come from a place of fear and I actually had nothing to be afraid of by staying in mum's house.

A few days after Christmas, I sat down with mum and told her that I didn't want to move out and that I wanted to stay at home. She was pleased and there were a lot of hugs. I still hadn't been able to convey to mum what I had been afraid of. I called the guys that evening and told them that I would be staying at home. It was a difficult conversation, and they didn't seem to understand my point of view, but I made it clear that I was staying put. I knew that I still owed them the money for my flight, and I realised that I could afford to pay it straight off. I told mum that I wanted to take the money over to the guys, so mum and her boyfriend decided to take me over in his car the next morning on our way to visit my Nan.

I felt a little trepidation the following morning and I couldn't put my finger on why. We drove to their house, and I rang their doorbell. It took a while but one of them answered and it was 'the serious one.' I explained that I could afford to pay them back the money for the airline ticket. I handed over the envelope with the cash, he took it with a shocked look on his face and said we would speak later. There was no hug, no kiss on the cheek as usual, nothing. He just turned around and closed the door. I don't know what I was expecting, but that wasn't it!

We returned home later that afternoon, following our visit to my Nan's house. Tez had been at home all day, he told us that they had been to collect a couple of bits of furniture that we had borrowed from them a while back. There hadn't been any hurry to return them, they had said, so I guess we had just forgotten about them. Apparently, they hadn't, and they had chosen that afternoon, knowing that most of us would be out to collect them! That's when it hit me that I would never see them again.

I had been abandoned because I wanted to stick by my family! There was usually a lot of banter via text that took place, so I sent a text to say sorry that I had missed them when they collected the furniture. I received no reply at all, and I never heard from either of them ever again! A part of me was totally gutted but I also knew that the situation couldn't continue. I didn't want to lose my family and I hadn't realised that I had to make a choice and lose my friends too, but yes, apparently, that's exactly what had to happen. Weirdly, mum never mentioned them and what had happened over the last few months. Though, looking back now, I think mum was hurting too because they were her friends before they were mine, but she had fallen for her truck driver. Mum didn't take too kindly to bitchy comments and being made to feel like she had to choose her friends over her man.

Chapter Five – Moving out again!

I was beginning to get itchy feet back at home though. I loved my family dearly, but I had an independent streak, and I wanted my own space. I bumped into an old school friend at the bus stop one day. We began hanging out again, she was always fun to be around. She had a boyfriend who was also great fun.

She worked part time at a pub at the weekends, whilst he worked as a bouncer at another bar in the City Centre. They both had day jobs during the week too, but they were saving for a place together. I liked her boyfriend, he was funny and at the weekends, I would go and hang out at the pub where she worked and later, we would go onto the bar where he was working as a bouncer and have a drink or two there before closing time.

One night, they were both off and somehow, I ended up being set up on a Saturday night on a double date with one of his friends. My friend applied all my eye make-up before we went out as that has never been my thing. We all had a great time and I ended up a bit drunk. My date was driving and being sensible.

He dropped my friend and her boyfriend off at his place, which left me and him in the car. The booze had left me feeling a little bolder than usual.

I told him that I liked him, and I knew that he liked me as he had been touchy feely all night. I made it clear that I wanted him that night. He had his own place being a few years older than me, so we drove there.

You may remember that technically, I was still a virgin. I didn't know how to tell this guy and I was too tipsy to consider this properly as an option by this point. We began to have sex and of course it hurt, and I realised that I had made a mistake. He asked me if I wanted him to stop and I said yes. He did, and he was actually really good about it. I felt embarrassed, I was also pretty drunk, so I just began to cry and ended up blabbing about the breakup with my ex-boyfriend and him fancying Britney Spears! Yeah, I must have been pretty drunk!

A couple of weeks had passed, and I hadn't told my friend the full story about what had happened between me and her boyfriend's mate. I didn't dare to ask if he had said anything to my friend's boyfriend. I wasn't totally sure about how much guys talked amongst themselves.

Another weekend arrived and again, the three of us ended up at the bar where my friend's fella was working as a bouncer. Again, I was tipsy and feeling bold. There was a lot of banter between me and the bar manager who happened to be another friend of my friend's boyfriend! They went home and the bar manager said that he would drive me home. I was happy to accept the lift, so I told them to go on.

The bar manager locked up behind them and within seconds, we were kissing passionately! The disco was still on, so he decided to turn the disco lights on, I think it was an attempt to add some romance to the situation or something like that! We got intimate at the bloody bar! I liked this guy. He had been pretty funny, and the sex was okay. By the Monday morning, I felt atrocious and had to miss work. I had contracted tonsilitis. I texted my friend, she knew exactly what had happened on the Saturday night. She texted me back that the guy I'd had sex with had tonsillitis too! She also told me that he had a bloody fiancée! I was gutted, I felt like death warmed up and I had been used by someone I could never have for myself. I had recently found out that the first guy I had slept with weeks before, had also got a girlfriend at the time I went home with him.

I realised that alcohol seriously impaired my judgement and that I was developing a slightly slutty streak and that wasn't who I was! My friend's fella also begged me to stop sleeping with his friends! I didn't really have much of a social life after that, I didn't feel right becoming this drunken slut! I still continued to see my friend during the week though as she only lived round the corner from my mum's house.

One day, she said that her, and her

boyfriend, were looking for a place together. She suggested that the three of us look for a house share. She was worried that she would be a little lonely as he had several jobs working late hours so she could use the company with me around. I agreed, her boyfriend was a laugh, and I couldn't afford a place of my own. I was only working for a temp agency, so it made financial sense. We found a three-bedroom place with a garage link and a conservatory. It wasn't as grand as that sounds trust me! The conservatory was made of corrugated plastic and was a bit damp, but we could banish her boyfriend out there to smoke with his friends, as he smoked weed it later transpired!

The third bedroom was tiny so this was mainly a dumping ground for stuff that we couldn't fit into our bedrooms. The garage was also more of a storage space than anything else. The three of us got on quite well, he was at work a lot, so it was mainly me and my friend in the evenings. The two of us cooked and we gave him a lot of extra food. We weren't so good at the domestic stuff and so the house ended up a mess a lot of the time, but we weren't bothered by it!

We still needed a decent sofa, so my friend and I went to a sofa shop, and we ordered a sofa on credit. I took the credit agreement in my name. Next, we decided that we needed a decent stereo because every house needed a stereo! Again, it was purchased on credit in my name, and she would give me half the money every month to pay towards the credit payments.

I was working for a conveyancing firm in a temporary role, and I absolutely hated it! I decided that I needed a little extra money, so I took a role as a barmaid in a night club at the weekend. I quite enjoyed it apart from stinking of sweet and sticky spirits when I got home, as there was always at least one spillage during the night. The money I earned at the club paid my monthly share of the rent, so I was quite happy with that.

One weekend, the three of us had the weekend off from all of our jobs and we ended up at the bar where her boyfriend worked as a bouncer. Out of the corner of my eye, I noticed a guy that I knew from a previous job. He'd been a customer and I knew he had a girlfriend back then, but he was only with friends that night. He noticed me too and we went out the back, away from the crowd to chat. It was clear that there was a lot of chemistry between us!

He confessed that he was still in a relationship, so I backed off. I did tell him about the club that I worked in though! Thursday night arrived and I had a shift at the bar, I was feeling pretty rubbish as I was job hunting again. My role at the conveyancing firm had been ended by the agency and they didn't have anything else for me yet.

It wasn't that busy at the club and from nowhere appeared the guy that I had been chatting to at the bar the weekend before. He was with a couple of friends, and he said that he was bored as he was driving. He asked if he could drive me home at the end of my shift in a couple of hours. I told him that he could, and we arranged to meet out the front when I had finished.

My shift ended and I waited for a couple of minutes outside the club. I was nervous and I was wondering what the hell I had done; I hadn't had the chance to tell anyone that he was picking me up! He arrived and I got into his car. We had only gotten down the road when he pulled the car over. He told me that he liked me and that he knew there was chemistry between us. I nodded in agreement and then he suggested that we should have one night together, no strings attached and enjoy ourselves and the chemistry between us.

It turned out that I didn't need alcohol to decide to be naughty! He stayed the night and left the next morning. My housemates hadn't heard a thing so were keen to understand the reason for my particularly sunny disposition that morning as it was most unlike me! I told them, he wasn't overly bothered but she told me that as long as I had enjoyed myself and taken precautions then not to overthink it. So that was how I thought of it, a great night and I told myself that I wasn't harming anybody. Whether that was the case for him or not, I don't know as I never saw or heard from him again. Looking back, I still have good memories, but it perhaps wasn't such a proud moment, and it wouldn't be the last time that I would pursue those who were attached.

One night, my friend and I were talking. She was fed up working two jobs and I hadn't yet secured a new full-time role. We decided that we would set up a business together! We were so excited, and I was not in the mood to consider any of the pitfalls about going into business with a friend. We couldn't get a business loan, mostly due to the lack of a proper business plan. All that financial stuff has never been my thing and it certainly wasn't hers!

I was able to take out a personal loan in my name, she promised that she would help with the repayments. The loan was for just over £10,000 which was the maximum that they would lend me. 'Nitecrawler Enterprises' was born! We formed a dance agency that would supply dancers to clubs, and we'd run entertainment nights with strippers and provide clubs with DJ nights. We'd also have kissogram dancers on the books too.

We secured ourselves an office rental as we couldn't cope with working from home with the amount of people that we were meeting and dealing with, and we got flash new mobiles for work purposes. We took free business courses at the *Princes Trust*. She had a lot of contacts in the dance world and things were beginning to look up. We agreed to supply a couple of free dancers on a few Friday nights to one particular event. This wasn't put into a formal contract, I later discovered, as I understood that if things worked out after a couple of weeks, they would begin to pay for our services. This was the first time that I began to doubt my business partner.

We decided that we would hold a proper launch party at a local bar. We arranged for limousines to collect us and our parents with champagne. We invited all our friends and family; we had leaflets printed and balloons with our logo on. It was a great night but all we got out of it was a big bill rather than any bookings or leads!

We arranged to hold a lady's night at another local bar. We printed the leaflets ourselves to save on costs and I designed them on the computer. We put leaflets everywhere that we were allowed to in the City Centre in the lead up to our event. We had absolutely no one turn up and we had to pay our dancers and our bouncers. I was beginning to doubt that we were ever going to get anywhere.

My business partner decided that we would branch out and also supply bouncers. Her boyfriend's brother-in-law was seeking work and he was appointed head bouncer at an event - the only problem was that he didn't own a decent suit. Behind my back, my friend took him shopping and bought him a suit with our/my money! I couldn't believe it and doubt really began to creep in. I was in charge of keeping tabs on our finances and all I could see was that we were haemorrhaging money and with no hope of getting any coming back to us.

Our next event was a club night at a bar with a late license. We had a DJ, who was a friend of her boyfriend, and we did our own marketing to save money. I was on the door that night collecting the entry fees. I had recently begun smoking again, and that night I chain smoked to help me deal with the abysmal reality of nobody turning up! That was more money paid out and with no return. My business partner always had the outlook that something was around the corner, and she was happy to see where things went. She never had a problem spending money either.

I had arranged a weekend away with a couple of friends in Blackpool to take time out to get away and think and just have some fun without any stress. That wasn't what happened! My business partner had assured me that she had an event planned and it was guaranteed to bring some money in, and it would pay the rent that was due on the Monday when I was due back from Blackpool.

Alarm bells were ringing in my head and as we pulled into Blackpool station, my phone rang. It was bad news, our landlord told me that our rent was due that day. I told him that we had an event that weekend and that he would have the money on Monday morning when we thought that it was due. He reminded me of our rental agreement and that I had got the dates wrong. I told him I was away, and my business partner was organising the event. He seemed placated for the time being.

Things got worse over the weekend, I had gotten drunk and had a blistering hangover for most of the Saturday. The event had fallen through for reasons that weren't totally clear to me because my business partner was not answering my calls. I can't remember the number of times that I had called her compared to how many times she had answered me and fobbed me off. We were in dire straits; we couldn't afford the rent payment or any of our other bills. Our business was over! We had also been living on my credit card to pay our other expenses and we had socialised a lot too.

On my return to Leicester, we had a frank and honest discussion about the business and the state of our finances, both personal and business. In short, we were broke, and all the debt was in my name! With the business loan, my credit card, the sofa and the stereo, the total was about £23,000! I was heartbroken and bloody angry!

My friend had no idea and displayed an incredibly dismissive attitude towards the debt. We argued a bit which got us nowhere. I shut down in my reaction to the shock and went to bed and had a good cry. I felt let down and stupid. I needed to get a job and soon.

The next morning, we received a letter from our office landlord. He had changed the locks on the building. All our equipment including our computer was still in there. I had a legal contact from an evening course that I had undertaken a couple of years before. She informed me that our landlord had acted illegally and that he should have taken certain steps before changing the locks and seizing our equipment.

She also told me that we were at liberty to gain entry to the building and get our equipment as long as we informed the police of what we were doing and why.

We had a friend, whose dad was quite handy with a van and a lot of power tools. The tools included an angle grinder and a very long extension lead. There was a pub on the corner of the street, and he was confident that if they would allow us to plug the extension lead into their power, it would stretch all the way down the street, and he'd be able to remove the new padlock.

We were a little over excited at this thought! I had tried to reason with the landlord, but he was adamant that he would not allow us into our office to obtain our property. I called the police the day that we intended to get our things. They had no issue with it, and they thanked me for informing them. We were going to commit authorised burglary!

We arrived outside the office, and we took the extension lead down the road to the pub. It had been a regular haunt for us over the previous few months, so they knew us well. The owner was more than happy to assist when we told her what had happened. It must have looked a bit odd, a wire trailing all the way down the street! But once the angle grinder was connected, it took less than thirty seconds to cut through and remove the padlock.

The main lock hadn't been changed and the alarm code was still the same. We grabbed our equipment and emptied our office. I left the keys on the stairs for the landlord and pulled the door closed behind us before we scarpered. We never heard from him again thankfully!

Back at the house, we were a little high on adrenaline, hardly believing what we had been allowed to do! We unloaded all our stuff, and we knocked back a couple of drinks before we went to bed. The next morning the reality hit home. We owed two months' rent on the house, I had about £23,000 in debt in my name and we had no money.

We discussed our options and again, my so-called friend was pretty non-committal about any of it. We agreed that we would sell our equipment including the laptop to raise some funds. I took that and some other stuff into town to the local market to sell, hoping to get some money towards the rent that we owed. I didn't even get enough to cover one month, let alone two! I realised that all this debt was on me, I needed to get a job and I needed to get out of that house! And fast!

I went to see my mum who worked in a shopping centre so I was hopeful that she would have a moment to talk. Luckily, she wasn't busy, and I told her everything and about all the debt. She was shocked but thankfully sympathetic. When she asked if I wanted to come home, I was so grateful! I told her that I couldn't afford to transport all my things back home so mum kindly offered to pay for that too.

I went back to the house, and my friend was giggling on the phone. I couldn't believe it; how could she be in such a good mood? I told her that I was moving out, that I couldn't afford to live there anymore and that I needed to sort the debts out as they were all in my name. We argued when it became clear that she and her boyfriend would have to sort the rent out. I told her to get herself sorted out with a job and that it would be nice if she could help pay some of the debt off as she helped to spend it! Over the next few days, we avoided each other. I packed up my things and that weekend, a Man and Van helped me transport me and my belongings back to mum's. I was twenty-two years old and back to square bloody one and completely broke!

Chapter Six – Back at mum's yet again and oh, more madness!

I wasn't one to hang about though - I registered with a recruitment agency who placed me at the local council in their HR Department. I also registered with a debt repayment agency who helped me to reduce the amount I would be paying out. I worked out that based on the repayments and the amount that I owed, it would take about two hundred and sixty-four years to pay it all back! My outgoings were; the rent I paid to mum, bus fare to and from work and a few toiletries. My life was work and home, I had no money for anything else, but in some ways, this felt like my penance for being so stupid and trusting.

My former housemate/business partner had offered to pay me some money towards my debts, but she never actually came through with the cash. I later heard that she and her boyfriend had moved out of the house and that she had sold the sofa and the stereo that I was still paying for! I gave up contacting her and she never contacted me. I did receive around a thousand pounds from her eventually after mum bumped into her and told her that she needed to do the right thing.

I settled back into life at mums. Her trucker boyfriend was still there, and things were going quite well between them. He was working as a long-distance lorry driver, so he was away at least one night per week. He and I developed a banter between us. I liked him a lot and he was good to mum and to me.

All of what happened had knocked the wind out of my sails, so I concentrated on work. My temp position at the Council was quite long term but they were unable to guarantee that a permanent position would become available. A local position came up at a Transport Company that was owned by a well-known bus company. I was sorry to leave my colleagues at the council, but it was time to move on.

My new role was different again, I became a Purchase Ledger Clerk. The company were not particularly advanced with their technology. I had to number the invoices that came in with a numbered handstamp, which was quite hard on the wrists I can tell you! I logged the invoices into a book rather than on an accounts system. The role was monotonous, but it was permanent, and I needed the money. After a while though, I began to have some real problems with my hands, to the point that I could barely pick up a pen! I had to take some time off and the doctor sent me for some tests.

I assumed that it was repetitive strain injury but with my dad having arthritis, that was at the back of my mind. I hadn't been sleeping too well either or very often I would sleep but I felt like

I had never been to bed. I had a lot of other pains too. I tried at work to write with my left hand, but as a right-hander, my writing was totally illegible! At one point, I dropped a kettle full of water. Luckily this was before the kettle had boiled so I was uninjured! Eventually, I was referred to Rheumatology at the hospital. I had no markers for Rheumatoid Arthritis in my blood tests, so the GP was slightly bemused.

The Rheumatologist diagnosed me with Fibromyalgia. The doctor's words were something like "it could have been worse." That didn't make me feel any better! He gave me a leaflet about fibromyalgia and sent me on my way. I went home and read the leaflet and my diagnosis made sense at last!

However, fibromyalgia was still an unknown and misunderstood condition. There were no particular reasons for the condition or so they thought at the time, nor any medications beyond the usual paracetamol or ibuprofen.

I found a local support group which took place monthly at the local hospital. I was the youngest person in the room at twenty-two, I couldn't believe it! They were a lovely bunch of people but, they were all so much older than me.

That first meeting devastated me and made me feel so much worse physically for at least a week. It was becoming clear to me that my mental state impacted my physical state. I knew that I needed to understand my condition better, so I attended the next meeting and to most meetings after that.

It was nice to know that I wasn't the only one with the condition and I did learn some techniques to help. One lady gave me a hand, neck, and shoulder massage with a guided meditation that I have never forgotten. I don't know how long it had lasted but I felt like I had been to sleep for a week! I have never found a meditation or masseuse that has had that effect since!

Eventually though it became obvious that I could not continue with my purchase ledger job. I was so tired a lot of the time and the writing and stamping were killing my hands. I began to look for other roles and I was lucky enough to secure a part time role at the local hospital. This was as a recruitment administrator for one of the Departments. I would be working until mid-afternoon along with one full-time lady. We got on well and between us we had the recruitment completely organised.

I was out shopping with mum one weekend, when we heard a familiar voice shout "Vonnie, over here!"

We turned around to see my dad gesturing wildly from the entrance to a café. I won't lie, my first thought was "oh shit, what does he want?" mum looked at me with a look that demonstrated that she knew exactly what I was thinking and said, "come on, we might as well see what he wants."

I wasn't sure but we both went over to the cafe, and he beckoned us inside to his table. He bought us a cup of tea and we sat and chatted for a while. He seemed to be in a good mood, and this felt different to all the other times that I had seen him over the years. I gave him my number and we discussed meeting up again on our own. I came away feeling weird - that is the only way that I can describe it. Things between dad and I had always been difficult and by this point, our relationship had been broken for more than a decade. Mum sensed that I was in a weird headspace. She hugged me when we got home and said, "It will be okay you know?" I hoped that she was right, but I wasn't quite ready to share her faith.

Dad and I did meet up again, just a couple of weeks later. We went to the pub which was no surprise really. I was an adult though and I enjoyed a drink or two myself! Things between us were easier but dad talked a lot when he had a drink, and we had the best part of a decade to catch up on. Soon enough, I was staying at dad's flat over the weekends on a sofa bed in the living room. My brother and I would generally alternate weekends as there wasn't room for the both of us.

When I stayed over, we'd start at the pub before going back to his place. I didn't get to bed until 3am some nights because dad wouldn't shut up talking! I discovered that I had a taste for bitter one weekend during a pub visit, albeit in lesser amounts to my dad. I quickly realised that whilst I wanted and appreciated having dad back in my life, I could not keep up with his drinking. His sofa bed was also killing my back and hips and it didn't help that I couldn't take my meds when I was drinking with dad either.

Instead, I began to see him on Saturdays or Sundays, admittedly at a pub, but this allowed me to go home when I had reached my limit. Sometimes mum would join us, and we would share a bottle of wine. Sometimes Tez was there too, and we had a nice family atmosphere for a good long while.

Soon I turned twenty-four and things were going relatively well. I had a job that I enjoyed, the hours worked well for me, and home life was pretty settled. I was seeing dad regularly and that was working out. You could say that I had become a bit of a daddy's girl again.

As always though, drama was never far away from me. My second cousin began spending a lot of time at our house. He had lived with us for a while when I was eleven or twelve, so there was a closeness between us all. He had often acted as babysitter whilst mum was out.

By this point though, he had been married for about four or five years and the marriage was crumbling. She apparently had fallen out of love with him. Truthfully though, I'd had feelings for my cousin since I was about sixteen years old. I had pushed my feelings down though in order to forget about him. This time though, it was a damn sight harder. We ended up spending a lot of time together, he would pick me up and take me to work or pick me up and bring me home. He worked for a food delivery company, so he worked weird hours, and he didn't want to be at his house because things were so bad with his wife.

One morning he took me to work, and we were chatting. He said something about always liking me and how much we got on. I replied with 'yeah, I've always thought of you as a brother.' I couldn't believe that sentence had come out of my mouth!

I walked into my office, my work colleague saw my face and she knew that something was wrong! She knew that I had feelings for him, and she told me that I needed to be honest with him about how I felt. I knew that she was right, but I could not believe that I had said such a stupid and untrue sentence! I didn't hear from him or see him for a few days which made me feel a whole lot worse. Mum knew that something was wrong, but I couldn't tell her the truth. She would be angry, and she had enough to deal with as my Grandad, her dad, had become very sick.

My cousin turned up at our house that weekend and he sat and watched a film. I enjoyed a smoke so we both stepped outside for a cigarette in mum's back garden. We talked and the conversation came around to what was said a few days before. I told him that was a stupid comment I'd made and that wasn't how I really felt. Before I knew it, we were kissing. I was giddy!

I couldn't believe that he felt the same way! We arranged to meet up the next day and he went home. I knew that this was going to be difficult as already mum wasn't keen on us spending so much time together. I didn't think that she would approve but I didn't care either. There was also the matter of him still being technically married too. I went to bed, but I was too excited to sleep!

The next day, I told mum that I was going out with him for a drive. Mum scowled at me as she said, 'you two are spending a lot of time together. Do you want his wife to cite you in the divorce proceedings?'

I scowled back as I replied, 'he's my cousin, what's the problem with that?'

I could see mum wasn't satisfied with my answer, but I was twenty-four years old, and I didn't feel like I had to justify my movements to my mother. I was beginning to feel like I might need to move out again and soon! He picked me up round the corner as I had texted to warn him not to come to the house to get me. We continued to see each other over the coming weeks. Mum became more suspicious, but I had fallen for him, and I wasn't in the mood to listen to her.

He and his work colleagues were arranging a night out one Saturday in a town not far away from Leicester. He asked if I would like to go, and we could stay over in a bed and breakfast. I jumped at the chance. We knew mum would hit the roof, so I told her that I was going away with a friend from work. Mum had not met my friend before and said friend did not have my contact details so I was pretty sure that she wouldn't be able to drop me in it with mum. It all seemed fool proof and it only added to the excitement.

I did what any girl does when she knows that she will be having sex with her boyfriend for the first time - I went shopping for underwear! The weekend of our adventure dawned, I waved goodbye to mum and caught the bus to our meeting point in the city centre. I was beyond excited! We had nearly been caught fooling around a few days before at his house. We hadn't gone the whole way but luckily, he had left his key in the front door. We had just gotten dressed and come downstairs when his wife knocked at the door!

I scurried into the living room and collected my coat and bag as she came into the room. We made small talk before he mumbled something about taking me to a job interview. I nodded and mumbled my goodbyes to her. I honestly hadn't been able to get out of the house fast enough!

We arrived at our B&B for the night and

checked in. It was nice, nothing special, but we got ready to go out and have dinner before meeting his work colleagues. We had just been seated when I heard the message alert sound on my phone. I unlocked my phone and found the message from mum. As I read it, I realised that the game was up. She made it clear that she knew exactly where I was and who I was with and just how furious she was with us both. His phone pinged; he had received a similar message from mum too.

We looked at each other, I was blinking back tears. I hated confrontation and this situation could kill our relationship and I didn't want that to happen. He asked me what I wanted to do, so I took a breath and told him that I loved him and that I didn't want this to affect us. He told me that he wanted to stand by me and our relationship. I texted mum back and told her that yes, she was right, I was with him and yes, we were a couple. We went back and forth with our texts for a while before I told her that I wouldn't be speaking to her again until the next day and that I would be turning my phone off.

We ate our dinner, and we went to the pub to meet his work colleagues. We both had a few drinks. We needed them as we didn't know what we were going to face the next day when we got back. We staggered back to our B&B. We'd had a laugh with his work colleagues, but they were a bit loud and laddish for me. We reached our room, and we began to kiss and undress each other. This was the whole point of our weekend after all!

The sex was pleasant enough, I wasn't particularly experienced, but it was a little quicker than I would have liked. Knowing that we were going to be facing a storm of fury the following day, I was looking for cuddles and reassurance after the first time we'd had sex. I didn't get that; he rolled over and went to sleep! I couldn't sleep that night, I wanted to know how he felt about me. Did he see a future for our relationship? My brain was on overdrive. Had I been too easy? Was this just going to be a one-night stand? Eventually, I think my brain got sick of my barrage of thoughts and I gave into sleep.

The next morning, I was quiet at breakfast and as we returned to the room to pack up our belongings, he asked me what was wrong. I confessed that I was scared. I told him that mum had sent more messages since the night before and I was scared how things were going to go with her. I told him that I was scared our relationship was over because of this. He held me and said that we would face mum together and that he would stand by me no matter what. I'd had feelings for him for so long that I couldn't give him up just because mum didn't approve. I hadn't cost him his marriage because they were splitting up and divorcing anyway.

We decided not to go straight home, we

thought that we would give mum some time to simmer down and neither of us were ready to face her to be honest. We went to the cinema; the film was atrocious, and we were both as tense as hell!

After the film, we knew that we had to face the music and neither of us wanted to, but we went back anyway. I gingerly opened the front door with my key - mum had clearly not simmered down. The living room door burst open; mum appeared with a thunderous look on her face.

'Where the hell have you been?' she roared.

I think I jumped a little at the ferocity of her voice, I had never heard her like that before I swear! I mumbled about having sent a text about coming home a little later.

'You both need to get in that room and tell me what the fuck is going on with you two!' She roared again.

I was afraid, again I mumbled that I wasn't doing anything wrong and that we needed to have a civil conversation about it all. Before I knew it, mum's boyfriend had grabbed hold of me and dragged me into the living room whilst calling me a "stupid girl." I was shoved onto the sofa; my brother was also in the room looking suitably unimpressed. My boyfriend came and sat next to me, and I could feel his tension too. I felt sick as mum started to rant at us.

The upshot of it was, she was furious with

us for being together because we were cousins. I reminded her that second cousins in a relationship was perfectly legal. His wife now knew, and she was also livid. I couldn't understand why, she had been talking about a divorce for weeks anyway. Most of all, mum was furious at us for lying to her. It was very clear from the beginning of us spending more time together that mum had a big issue with us being in a relationship, so we had taken the coward's way out.

I was also told that my dad wouldn't be happy, and that dad knew people who could hurt us. Dad was well into his 60s and I knew that he liked to talk himself up a lot, so I doubted this massively. Mum was still shouting and basically told me that we had to break our relationship off if I wanted to continue to live at her house. I saw red this time and threw my keys at her yelling about not being controlled and stormed off upstairs to get my suitcase! I quickly packed as many of the basics as I could fit into my case. Mum was in the room before I knew it and her voice was getting more high-pitched by the minute. Hurriedly, I zipped it up and began dragging it downstairs.

My boyfriend was waiting for me and took my case from me. Mum was still yelling at the top of her voice, and she reached the bottom of the stairs. She asked my boyfriend why he was being so quiet, but when he did go to speak, she punched him in the stomach! He doubled over. I opened the front door and as we left, mum hurled the DVDs that he had left at the house at our heads. She missed and they flew past our ears as she wasn't a very good shot.

We got into his car and drove off. I was in tears, and I had no idea where the hell I was going to sleep that night. We saw a cash machine, so we pulled over and withdrew all that I had in my account. We drove to his dad's house and when we walked in, it was clear that he'd had a phone call from mum. His first words were 'well, you two have put the cat amongst the pigeons.'

I tried to smile but I was still crying. We sat down, hand in hand, and my new boyfriend explained what had happened and that I had walked out of mum's house. My Great Uncle pulled out the local newspaper and began looking for listings of rooms to rent and local bed and breakfast places. I explained that I didn't feel safe as mum had promised us that his ex-wife's relatives were out looking for us. I later learned that this wasn't true but, in that moment, I felt scared. My boyfriend worked at an industrial estate outside the city and there was a pub with a hotel around the corner from his work. It was agreed that we would stay there, and it meant that he could still go to work whilst we got sorted out. Of course, now his wife knew, he was now homeless too!

We promised to keep in touch with my

Great Uncle and we left. We reached the pub, and they had a room available for two nights, relieved, we booked in. Once we reached our room, my tears had finally subsided, but I felt angry and confused. I couldn't believe what the hell had happened and how in the blink of an eye my life had been turned completely on its head.

We sat on the bed to talk, and he put an arm around me. He told me that we were in this together and we kissed and ended up making love. As we got ready to sleep, he told me that he loved me. I will admit to thinking that he could have told me that before we'd had sex, but I was glad that he had feelings for me. I do acknowledge however, that he may have felt that he'd had little choice but to make promises now that he had nowhere to go either as we had been caught out.

The next morning, I woke up alone. He had to be at work for some god-awful hour. I sent a text to my boss to let her know what had happened and that I wouldn't be at work for a couple of days. She was shocked but kindly agreed to the time off. I spent most of the day scared in case his wife's relatives did manage to find us. He came back to the hotel sometime in the afternoon with a local paper in his hand. We scoured for somewhere to stay.

There was a bed and breakfast in Leicester City Centre. We called them and they had a room that would be free from the following evening. We could just about afford it for the next few weeks. We couldn't afford another night in the hotel that we were already in, so his dad said that we could stay at his for the night. There wasn't room for it to become a long-term arrangement, but we were grateful for the one night.

As we were moving to the bed and breakfast, his dad said that we could cook our dinners at his house so that we could save some money. We cooked a lot of Spaghetti Bolognaise in those weeks I can tell you! Once we had moved some of our stuff to the bed and breakfast the following afternoon, we worked out a budget for food over the coming weeks.

We kept a few basic supplies in our room - we practically lived off peanut butter sandwiches for lunch! Our menu was very basic, but we at least had cigarettes too! (Don't judge!) I went back to work the next morning, my boss was very concerned, but I assured her that I was okay and that my boyfriend was standing by me.

I had only been back in the office for ten minutes when my work phone rang. I answered it to find a very familiar voice at the other end - it was dad. He wanted to know what had happened as mum and my brother had called him a few times. Dad reassured me that he loved me and that if I was happy that was all that mattered. I had tears in my voice as we said goodbye. At least dad was still talking to me.

Less than twenty minutes later, my work phone went again, it was mum this time. The first thing she asked was if I was still talking to her. I told her that depended on whether she planned on screaming at me again. She told me that she wasn't. We agreed to meet and go for a cup of tea in town when I finished work.

I was nervous waiting for her and as she approached me, it was clear that she was nervous too. We hugged and cried a little and we sat in a café to talk. I made it clear that we were now a couple, that I was not moving home and that we were temporarily living in a bed and breakfast in town. Her anger had subsided at least. I told her that dad had called me, and we had arranged to have lunch that weekend.

I went back to my boyfriend's dad's house for dinner before we both went back to the B&B. I told him about the latest developments, he was pleased that relations were being restored with my family. Over the next few weeks, we had a bit of a routine which kept us going. The B&B was a bit grubby, but it did us.

I saw dad a few times, he made a point of telling me that he was proud of me for standing my ground and for surviving in a B&B. I was happy to hear this but surprised to be hearing it from my dad. I saw mum a few times too, but I had to go by myself as my boyfriend wasn't yet welcome. My Grandad's health had deteriorated so I was able to see him a few times too. My Nan wasn't entirely thrilled by our new relationship by all accounts, but Grandad needed family around him.

We were at the B&B for about a month until we both got paid from our jobs. We noticed an advert in the local paper for a house share. We figured it would only be a little while until we could afford a flat together. He had child maintenance to consider as well as legal fees, now his ex-wife had begun divorce proceedings against him.

The house share had about ten people including us. There was one bathroom to cover nine people as one room had an ensuite. There was a cleaner who came twice a week. The kitchen was always a mess though which regularly infuriated me.

My Grandad quickly went downhill shortly after we had moved into the house. I had been able to see him the week before, but he was now in a hospital bed being tended to by MacMillan Nurses twice a day. It was Easter Bank Holiday weekend, and the MacMillan Nurses hadn't arrived at Nan's house. Grandad was in so much pain according to mum's regular updates. He passed away early on the Saturday morning. I was alone when mum called and I was devastated. I called my dad as my boyfriend was at work all day and I didn't want to be alone.

Dad was awake and he told me to get myself

over to his. I was on his doorstep within the hour! He welcomed me in and stretched his arms out and I just collapsed into those arms and cried! Dad looked after me that day, he let me sleep in his favourite chair as I was pretty tired. He took me out for lunch at a local pub and he took me for a couple of drinks. We went back to his, before my boyfriend collected me late in the afternoon when he had finished work. This was a sad day because Grandad had died, yet it still remains the day that I felt closest to my dad. I think perhaps it was because my defences were down, and I was able to let him care for me for once.

Dad had listened to me talking about the house share and how much I hated it. He told me that if we could find a flat with rent that we could afford, he would lend me the deposit. I was flabbergasted to say the least! I was trying to make my own way and dad had wanted to help his daughter out. I was very grateful for dad's offer.

Once Grandad's funeral had taken place, we found a flat in a converted Victorian house in a nice area of Leicester. Dad lent us the deposit as promised. The flat was fully furnished so we only needed the basics such as plates, cups, cutlery, and towels which was a massive help financially. The flat was lovely if a little too grand to be fair. We were happy there, but it did mean that I had to get another job with more hours to help pay the bills. I accepted a HR Administrator role that was full time at 40 hours per week.

Mum had by this point, forgiven us both and she was a regular visitor at the flat. I kept getting tonsilitis every month, so eventually, the doctor agreed to refer me to have them removed. I had to take time off work to recover from the operation though, as with fibromyalgia it always takes me a long time to recover from even a simple cold. The long hours at work coupled with my fibromyalgia meant that I began to get ill quite frequently unfortunately.

There was also the issue of dad. He became quite ill and with our newfound closeness, I took on the responsibility of looking after him. His mental health had always been quite up and down, but by now, he wasn't doing well at all.

He called me and told me that he hadn't eaten for four days and had no food in the house. He also didn't want to leave the house to get any food. I was shocked and called mum. She agreed to meet me after work to go over and sort him out. We went over, did some shopping for him, and made him a sandwich. However, he wasn't in a good way at all, so I called his psychiatrist who advised me to call the mental health crisis team. They assessed that he wasn't a risk to anyone, and they would make regular appointments to see him. I don't know if that happened or not to be honest.

I went to dad's every weekend and did his

weekly shopping for him and paid his bills too. He would often ring me at all hours of the day, and I can't function on little sleep. One week, I was on my lunch break when dad called. His medication was ready to collect from the pharmacy which was a ten-minute walk from his bungalow. He refused to go and get them. I couldn't go due to my working hours and by the time I got there, the pharmacy would have closed.

I called mum, who agreed to go and pick them up and drop them at dads. In time, dad's mental health got much worse and sadly, he turned on me! He accused me of stealing items or money from his bungalow. Things which he hadn't had in his possession for some years according to my brother. He would call me filthy names over the phone - I didn't know how to cope with any of this as it felt so personal. Then one day, I broke!

I called his Community Psychiatric Nurse in tears during my lunch break. I told her everything that dad had said to me and admitted that I just couldn't take any more. She was so lovely and explained that dad probably wouldn't remember any of this, and he likely didn't mean any of it. But she knew about our difficult history so she totally understood my reasoning for taking a step back because I just could not cope any longer. I posted all of dad's bills and payment books along with my keys through his door.

The nurse agreed to see him more regularly and she agreed that she would try to explain why I wouldn't be seeing him for a while. Within weeks of my stepping back, dad had to be sectioned. He had apparently been sleeping with a kitchen knife and had upended his settee across the doorway. He kept saying to his nurse that someone had moved it - no one could get in to move it! I was called as a courtesy whilst I was at work on a Friday afternoon. I felt like such a bitch for agreeing to the sectioning order, but my brother didn't know either what to do for the best or how to cope with him. No one gives you a manual or even some idea on what can happen with these conditions!

Once dad had been assessed, he was diagnosed with bipolar disorder. I didn't understand the condition at all. I was under the impression that dad was schizophrenic. I didn't visit dad during his first sectioning, I was simply too hurt by the things that he had said so I left my brother to take fresh clothes up to him and spend time with him. I still needed to understand dad's illness. After watching a TV series on BBC One about bipolar disorder, finally, the jigsaw pieces slotted into place. The lows of not eating or being able to get out of bed, coupled with the highs of his latest episode was explained.

His drinking finally made sense; he was self-medicating. It was clear that the bipolar went back years and this was how he had been coping with the gremlins in his head. But, given the things that he had said and done to all three of us over the years, I still couldn't forgive or excuse him completely. I struggled to move past all that hurt, and I knew that there would never be any kind of apology because he either didn't remember or believe that he had done anything wrong.

Dad was in the psychiatric hospital for about six weeks. He was released with a prescription for mood stabilisers and anti-depressants and would be monitored by the Community Psychiatric Nursing Team. Dad being dad though, ignored the advice of the doctors about his drinking and he continued to be a regular at his usual haunts.

I kept an eye on him from a distance and I would check in with the odd pub landlord around the city to see if he had been in. His visits had lessened, and one landlord told me that he had been banned because "he was a fucking nuisance!" I understood his reasoning as when dad was drunk, he was damn difficult to deal with. Add his medications into the mix and he could go from reasonably placid and drunk to ready for a fight over the slightest thing despite walking with two crutches!

My brother called me a couple of days after my chat with the landlord. He hadn't been able to get hold of dad; he wasn't at the bungalow either. I told him what had been said at the pubs. We gave him a couple more days to show up but there was still no sign of him. I decided to call the police and report him as a missing person. We didn't know what else to do, my boyfriend had driven around the streets in his neighbourhood, but he was nowhere to be found.

The police took all the details and promised to do what they could to find him. A few days later, I received a call from an unknown number. It was a lady who told me that dad was staying with her because he was unwell. I thanked her and took her address. I informed the police of dad's supposed whereabouts and they said that they would perform a welfare check.

They called me back a short while later to let me know that dad was fine if a little anxious. A few hours later, dad called me himself from the lady's phone. He was absolutely livid that I had called the police to find him. He didn't want to listen to my reasoning and that my brother was just as keen to find him as I was. He called me more filthy names before hanging up on me. Again, I was upset, and I just didn't know how to process this.

About a week later, the lady who dad was staying with called me again. She told me that dad was highly agitated and that he couldn't settle. She didn't know what to do and I told her that I certainly didn't, so I told her that I would call his CPN. His CPN agreed to go out and see dad, she fully knew about his case, and she had the qualifications and skills to deal with this type of situation. Whereas I only felt useless and was only capable of making dad angrier.

I received a call that evening to inform me that the Police had been called and dad had been sectioned again. I thanked the CPN, at least I knew that he was safe and being looked after. She encouraged me to go and see dad in a couple of weeks at the unit when the doctors had been able to tweak dad's meds. I told her that I would see, she understood my reticence after everything we'd gone through.

I had a decent couple of weeks with little drama, so I felt a bit more like myself, but guilt was clouding my thoughts. My brother told me that he was going to see dad with his girlfriend and their little boy who was about six months old. He asked if I would like to join them, and I agreed. As it was a group visit, I hoped that dad would be less likely to attack me verbally in front of others. It turned out to be a lovely visit; dad had loved seeing his little grandson and I agreed to go back again when I could.

Dad was released again but this time with a care plan. CPNs and carers would visit regularly and do his shopping for him and collect his medication from the chemist. They sometimes helped with cleaning too. This all took quite a weight off me so dad and I would meet for lunch every couple of weeks or so. Sometimes my brother would join us and occasionally mum would even come too. Every now and then, dad would dip again so we would visit him at the bungalow instead of having a pub lunch, I would take him a sandwich and a cake as my treat to him.

In time though, dad was leaving the bungalow less and less and we couldn't quite grasp why. He was a bit more on edge and became quite forgetful and took to repeating himself all the time. The next thing I knew, my brother told me that dad had been diagnosed with Alzheimer's disease. It was still early onset, but I had no clue what it meant or what was to come.

Dad started to go out again, but he would forget what day it was, that we had arranged to meet, or he wasn't aware of time at all. The CPNs were making more frequent visits and a key safe was installed at the bungalow. The carers were made responsible for giving dad his medications because he kept muddling it up. I don't remember what led up to it, but dad had to be admitted to a special unit for older people with conditions like Alzheimer's and Dementia.

He was assessed by an occupational therapist which happened to fall on a good day, and he was released back home with virtually the same care plan in place as before. Within days, he had to be readmitted to the unit. I was furious that he had been released so soon and no changes had been made to his care. I rang his CPN and begged for a meeting with the team responsible for dad's care and treatment as I felt that we were being given little information. Tez had his family to consider, and I understood and appreciated that, so I guess I ended up taking over more of the care and decisions which we tried to agree on between us.

When I attended the meeting, the occupational therapist was a twee little thing who told me dad had been able to make a cup of tea and operate his microwave. When I asked her if she had asked dad to read the instructions on a microwave meal and cook it accordingly, she said that no, she hadn't. I then told her that dad couldn't understand the instructions because he had put a frozen lasagne in the fridge, which defrosted it and then had cooked it for more than ten minutes, cremating the lasagne and melting the plastic. I told her that she had assessed him on a semi good day.

In the two days leading up to him being readmitted, he had lost his wallet twice. I had found it in the same place each time - under his pillow. He had lost the remote control twice, again I found it in the same place in his bedroom. Whenever he lost anything, he would call me in an absolute panic, and he wouldn't stop calling me until my boyfriend drove me over to his bungalow. The multi-disciplinary care team agreed to re-assess his care needs. This time, he was discharged, and the carers were instructed to cook his dinners and take him to the bank as necessary to withdraw his money for them to pay the bills on his behalf.

Chapter Seven - Something good for a change, or so I thought!

Everything with dad was working out nicely and there was less drama. My relationship with my boyfriend was going from strength to strength and he actually proposed to me at work! It was lovely, but it felt weird being the centre of attention in my workplace. Especially as my sickness rate at work had been unsurprisingly ridiculous! All the stress of dad had taken its toll on me.

Shortly after the proposal, I decided to begin job-hunting again. I was successful in my application to become a school receptionist at a private girl's school which was close to home. It was slightly less hours, more money and less of a commute. This was all good news for our wedding fund. I was quite thrifty and creative, so we started planning things on a budget.

We made our own invitations on the computer, and I made the wedding favours with supplies from a craft shop. My wedding dress was turquoise rather than white. We booked the town hall for a registry office wedding for July 2008. My now fiancé, had a terrible memory so we booked our wedding for his birthday to ensure that he never forgot our wedding anniversary! We booked a honeymoon in North Devon for a couple of days after the wedding.

Our wedding day passed in a blur, and I was on cloud nine! I was thrilled to become a wife and our relationship was for keeps after all that we had been through to be together. We had a small reception with approximately fifty friends and family. We were both so happy and I thought this was what love felt like. Our honeymoon in Devon was lovely and because we were on our honeymoon, our accommodation was upgraded! We did so many things that week, there was so much to see and do. Horse riding was scary yet amazing. I was a little annoyed though as my husband had gone off to the front of the group and I was left at the back on my own. We were on our honeymoon, and it would have been nice to have properly shared that experience!

Approximately four weeks later, I began to feel sick, and my period was late. I was pregnant! We were both so happy. It was confirmed by the doctor, and we made an appointment to see the midwife. With this being my first pregnancy, I didn't know that it was bad luck to tell people before the twelve-week scan.

However, I ended up feeling so sick that it was easy to tell! It wasn't just the ridiculous sickness though; I began to get severe neck and shoulder pains and I began to feel so tired and unable to cope that working each day was becoming impossible. The doctor signed me off sick to allow me some time to recuperate. I had stopped taking my fibromyalgia medication before I got pregnant and all I was allowed to take for pain relief was paracetamol.

I was excited about becoming a mum but nervous. I had never been particularly maternal, but my husband had a little boy from his first marriage, and I had begun to get the pangs for a child of my own. We had moved to a two-bedroom house so that we had a room for the baby. One night, I was just getting ready for bed, and I went to the toilet. I noticed a small amount of blood as I wiped. I told my husband and we rushed to the hospital. They examined me but I needed a scan, so I was booked in for the next day. I had to wait thirty-six hours to find out what was going on! It was a long day and we both tried to keep distracted until the scan.

I still felt pregnant, but the sickness had miraculously subsided as had the neck pain and that night, I had the best sleep that I'd had for a while. The morning of the scan arrived, and we eagerly went along to the maternity unit. We sat in the waiting room with the other expectant parents. I felt different somehow.

We were called in for my scan. We were told that the baby had no heartbeat. We were both utterly devastated but my husband tried to be strong for me. We were told that I had suffered a 'missed miscarriage' and I was booked in for an appointment four days later to take a tablet which would allow the foetus to detach and pass out of my body.

We went to my mum's, and I collapsed into her arms and sobbed my heart out. We began to make calls and tell the rest of the family. I went to bed for a while to rest, I was exhausted and getting sick of hearing the cliches from everyone such as "perhaps it was for the best" or "maybe the baby wasn't well enough to have a normal life."

Handy hint - when you are confronted by a person who has had a miscarriage just say that you are sorry for their loss and hug them! A few days later, my body decided to take care of the miscarriage itself. I was at home and suddenly I felt a whoosh down below. I rushed to the toilet and discovered that my pyjamas were covered in blood and the bleeding wouldn't stop. I was also in agony with cramps that I had never experienced before. My husband was at work, and I called him from the taxi to let him know where I was going. He promised to meet me there as soon as he could.

The maternity unit had to call a doctor down to reception with a wheelchair because I was in so much pain that I literally could not move. My husband arrived minutes later, and I was given a shot of morphine and placed on a commode behind a curtain with a receptacle to catch the contents. The morphine had barely time to kick in before another whoosh and that was it, no more pain and no more baby.

I climbed into bed and slept off the morphine, I was grateful to be numbed. I could barely speak to my husband; I just didn't know what to say. I woke a few hours later and I was informed that I was to be discharged as soon as the paperwork was ready. I felt fine if still a little dozy and hungry. I remember begging my husband to find me a cheese cob. I hadn't had much of an appetite over those few days after the scan.

I remained at home for another week until my sick note expired. On my return to work, I had a meeting with my boss. I wasn't coping and, in all honesty, I didn't want to be there, and I didn't feel that I fitted in with the other staff. My boss agreed to let me leave at the end of that week and with a full month's pay. My sickness record didn't look good, and I think that they just wanted rid of me. I didn't have a plan or another job to go to but people who know me know that I am not the kind of person to let the grass grow under my feet!

Within two weeks, I had a temporary position working at the local university. When it became available, I applied for the permanent role, and I was lucky enough to be appointed. There was a massive change in the role and the workload, and I realised that the job could be quite stressful.

Stress was becoming my perpetual state. We had only been living in our house for a couple of months when we decided to move in with my mum and stepdad. They wanted to get married and our rent would go towards their wedding fund. I loved my mum to bits so, in principle it was a good idea. We put all our furniture into storage.

Living at my mum's was hard for me. I like to have my own space occasionally and I wasn't getting that back there. Mum was constantly pointing out how untidy my husband was and to be fair she was right; he just didn't think about it. We had bickered over that since we had first moved in together, so I was fairly sure that he wasn't going to improve! I also began to notice just how bad he was with money.

I thought that with having less bills to pay, we would both be able to put some money into savings. How very wrong I was. By the second week of the month without fail, he would be broke. He was a smoker and a car owner, and it was often up to me to help him out financially. He would also ask his elderly dad for money too. I hated that he did that so I tried to give him as much as I could to stop him approaching his dad!

Within three months of living at mums, I had had enough! Dad could see the strain that it was taking on me, so he loaned us the money for a deposit on a two-bedroomed terrace house on the edge of the city. I did try to tell dad not to loan us the money, but he told me that it was a loan and that he couldn't watch me be miserable any longer. I was overjoyed to have more space again and in time to celebrate our first wedding anniversary that July.

It wasn't long before I was pregnant again. There were no neck pains but, work was massively stressful. I felt sick and exhausted all the time. We didn't tell many people this time as I didn't want to tempt fate. I had reached seven or eight weeks and again, there was a little blood when I went to the toilet. Again, we were told that there was no heartbeat, and we were both devastated all over again. I had been feeling little flutters from my belly during certain songs. I was gutted that again; I had lost the chance to become a mum.

This time, I opted for the operation to remove the foetus. The anaesthetic and pain took their toll on me, and the doctor signed me off for a week to allow me to recover. I felt depressed and exhausted but we still had a month before our first anniversary so my thoughts began to turn to how we could celebrate that.

One evening, my husband's work phone rang. Something just seemed 'off' about that call and his manner on the phone. He said that the alarm was going off at the Depot and as he was the Assistant Manager and the person nearest to the location, he would have to go and check that everything was okay. I said okay and settled on the sofa to watch a film while he changed into his favourite top and went on his way. About an hour later, he called me, and he sounded so weird on the phone.

I was told that a 'chap' was fixing the rear door as an intruder had tried to force it open but without success. You have to understand that my husband was my second cousin and so had been a part of my life for an incredibly long time and so I knew him better than I knew myself. He had never used the word 'chap' before in his entire life until that point and the way that he was babbling on, I just knew that something was wrong - I just couldn't put my finger on it…

He returned home about an hour after the phone call and there was still something 'off' about him. I tried to talk to him and ask if he was okay, but he just said that he was tired and wanted to go to bed as he needed to be up for work in the early hours as usual, so I didn't press him. However, I remained suspicious, and I knew the only place that I would find the truth of the matter would be on his phones.

I waited downstairs for about an hour until I heard him snoring. Both his work and personal mobile phones were on charge in the bedroom next to his side of the bed. I snuck up the stairs as quietly as I could and opened the door gently. He didn't stir, so quickly and quietly; I grabbed both of his phones and went back downstairs. I waited a few moments in case he got up but there was nothing but the sound of his snoring coming from upstairs. I unlocked each of the phones in turn and methodically began to check his emails, text messages and internet history. What I found shocked me to the core!

My husband of less than a year had been visiting gay dating websites and messaging men. He had been out that night to meet a man from one of the websites but, this man had apparently fallen asleep and didn't make their meeting which had been planned at my husband's depot! My husband was aiming to cheat on me with other men. I was still recovering from my second miscarriage, and we had been married less than a year - I simply couldn't process this shocking revelation. I couldn't keep a lid on how I was feeling either. I stormed upstairs with both his phones in my hand ready to confront him!

I angrily threw open the bedroom door and put the light on, he jumped out of his skin and asked, 'what's going on?'

I threw both his phones at him shouting that I knew what he had been up to and had seen the messages from the guy he was supposed to have met. He looked worried all of a sudden and he simply asked what I wanted to do. My reply was curt and to the point:

'I want you out of this house while I think. I can't look at you or even try to talk to you at the moment.'

He hurriedly got dressed and left for work

about two hours early. He told me that I could call him if I wanted to talk to him, I didn't reply and could only manage to grimace at him!

I charged back downstairs; it was about 11pm, but I was too wired or angry to sleep. Then an idea hit me that he may have used the laptop to start some of his searching. I checked the internet history after switching it on and he hadn't even cleared the internet history! I recognised the names of the websites that I had found on his phone. I clicked onto one and I clicked into the username box, and it came up automatically. I knew all his email passwords because my husband was always forgetting them, and he had used one of these passwords on the dating websites.

I was able to view his profile picture, an unflattering naked shot of him hanging out of one his work's lorries! I saw the types of men that he had searched for, mostly younger than him. Then I found the message section. I read them all and I was gobsmacked and disgusted all at once. Then the dates when some of the messages were exchanged hit me like a slap in the face! On the date that I was in hospital having the foetus removed after the miscarriage, it was clear that he had been messaging men after he had left me at the hospital to sleep for a while!

He had even been discussing his wife having a miscarriage so, he was making no secret about being married and nor were any of these men bothered! On checking his emails, there were more of the same and messages from another site, but these were more explicit in nature. It was clearly about hooking up for sex as opposed to looking for a relationship. I collapsed on the sofa and sobbed my heart out. Then I decided to call him. He answered on his blue tooth headset. I explained what I had found on my laptop and all he could muster up was to say sorry.

I was exhausted and I had nothing more that I could bring myself to say. Something made me log back into his emails and there was a new email from the guy that he had been due to meet that night. It was in reply to an email from my husband that he had sent seconds after we had spoken. My husband had told this man that his emails were being monitored by me. I couldn't take any more, so I took a sleeping tablet and went to bed.

I woke several hours later, still feeling exhausted both emotionally and physically. I managed to make some tea and breakfast. I didn't know what to do or what to think and I just stared aimlessly at the TV not knowing what I was watching. I felt broken, I couldn't keep a pregnancy and my marriage apparently was a sham. I knew that I couldn't talk to my mum about it all, she would want me to leave him and after everything that we went through to be together, I could not admit to her what he had done. I don't remember much about the rest of the day; I shut down and went into shock. Eventually, he came home, and he sat on the sofa next to me wanting to talk.

We tried to talk about what he had been doing. He confessed that he was confused about his sexuality, and he couldn't ignore it. He was sorry for hurting me and that he did really love me. I didn't know what to do, I just felt deeply ashamed and betrayed. I agreed to stay but I felt numb. Over the coming days, we tried to keep an open dialogue about his confused state of mind, but another emotion began to take hold. Anger! I was putting some clothes away a couple of days later and I found his favourite top. A red mist descended, and I found myself with the kitchen scissors in my hand and I cut that top into several small pieces and threw them down the stairs. When he came home and found them, he was not best pleased, and we argued. I think he was shocked by the level of my anger, but I had to just get it out of my system!

Things between us were uneasy for a while but I became more controlling than I ever thought was possible. I needed to know where he was constantly, and I secretly checked his emails for a long time afterwards. I tried to keep away from family as much as possible for a while because I knew that they would be able to tell that something was wrong. I was still not feeling myself either, the miscarriage coupled with this massive blow had truly knocked me for six.

About three or four months later, I had let things slip. I hadn't been checking his emails so often and he must have sensed this. Again, his behaviour became odd and, I checked his phones again. He had returned to the same gay dating websites again. We argued…again and I told him that I couldn't live as we were, and I would not be lied to. Either he was with me, or we split up so he could explore this side of himself.

I still wasn't strong enough to make the right choice for me in all honesty. He chose me. Thinking back though, I think that a lot of it was to do with the fear of his dad and his Victorian attitudes to homosexuality, which made me his safe bet.

Christmas was drawing close, and we had planned to stay at mum's house. Dad had been invited over for Christmas dinner and my brother would be there with his partner and his son. It was a lovely day mostly; my nephew was dressed in an adorable festive outfit, and he looked so cute! Later that day though, it became clear how unwell dad was now. He had gotten my brother confused with one of his own brothers, who had passed away. Dad began to get quite agitated so; we called his taxi a little earlier than we had planned to. We were all shook up by this, we knew it would happen but when it did, it felt like a huge kick in the gut!

The next morning, mum woke us up. My husband's uncle had succumbed to the cancer that he had been fighting the last few months. My husband went to collect his mum and they went to the hospital. He told me to stay at mum's as I didn't cope well with death. He drank several glasses of scotch that night which was unlike him but, I couldn't really blame him. The funeral took place a couple of weeks later, which was a slightly bizarre ordeal for us as his uncle was a Jehovah's Witness - and we were not!

Following the funeral, my husband was informed that he had been made executor of his uncle's will. He had a meeting with the solicitor, and it transpired that his uncle had left the house and its entire contents to my husband! We were in shock and totally grateful to his uncle. Was this to be our first step onto the property ladder?

The house was a bigger issue than we anticipated. It was an old, terraced house with no central heating or indoor toilet and not even a proper kitchen. Nobody would give us a mortgage and we couldn't just move in and renovate it slowly as I had fallen pregnant again. My husband was useless with money, not good at DIY and he had a job working very odd hours which meant that he was tired a lot of the time.

Realistically, the chances of him doing the renovations were nil. It took him a little time to accept this but, given that I had already been through two miscarriages, he didn't want this pregnancy to be any stress at all which I appreciated. We put the house up for sale as we didn't know what else to do with it. Luckily, it sold quite quickly. With the money, he paid off all our debts. I wasn't expecting him to pay mine off, but I was very grateful as I was still paying off all my earlier debts from the failed business with my friend.

Sadly, six weeks into my pregnancy, I found that I'd lost a little blood. This time though, the pregnancy hadn't developed enough to show what was happening or not happening. I had to go for weekly scans to monitor the foetal progress. By the third scan, the foetal pole (the thickening on the margin of the yolk sac of a foetus) had finally become visible. I was told that this was good news.

I went to work after the scan feeling hopeful. By that afternoon though, I started to experience brutal stomach cramps and when I went to the toilet there was a whoosh of blood. I knew then that my pregnancy was over. I called my husband, and he took me to the hospital. They had an emergency case, so I was kept waiting for quite some time. They finally agreed to admit me when it became clear that the bleeding was not going to stop, and my blood pressure had dropped to a dangerous low. They hooked me up to a drip. I wasn't even allowed to take myself to the toilet overnight in case I passed out in the toilet!

The next morning, I was given an internal scan which showed that the foetus was still there and so I was given an internal suppository to help it to detach itself and I was kept in hospital. I was prescribed some strong painkillers because the cramps were so painful. I finally passed the undeveloped foetus sometime that evening. Again, I spent a week resting at home as it was a busy period at work, and I just couldn't handle the stress. My mood was also incredibly low, and the slightest thing had me in tears. I felt useless and hopeless.

By the end of that summer, we decided to move house closer to my mum. We moved into a lovely three-bedroom semi-detached house. We ordered new furniture and we had it looking nice, I loved it! My husband decided to treat himself to a new car and we agreed that the money left over should be put into a bond as I knew that if we didn't put it somewhere safe, my husband would spend the lot!

On a night out with friends, I fell and hurt myself quite considerably, my husband took me to the hospital for an x-ray. I had very badly pulled all the muscles in both arms from the shoulders to the wrists! He drove me home, put me to bed and went to work. He had rung mum the next morning to look in on me. She was shocked when she did arrive because I couldn't even get myself out of bed or make a cup of tea for myself! She had to make my breakfast and feed me because I just couldn't do anything. My husband had left me alone in that state, if there had been a fire or any danger, I would have perished! I couldn't dress myself for almost a week and although my husband took a few days off work to look after me, his actions had left me questioning our marriage. Over that next two months, we bickered a lot!

On New Year's Eve 2010, I decided that I had just had enough and that we needed to have a big talk about everything before going into a new year. There were some arguments, but we did manage to talk and by the time that Big Ben had signalled the beginning of 2011, I felt that we were going to be okay. We spent New Year's Day at mums with the family, but we had work the following day so we didn't stay too late. I was beginning to feel hopeful that perhaps the drama that seemed to cling to my life might be slowly dying down. How very wrong I was…

Chapter Eight – A Marriage in Tatters

The next day, January 2nd, my husband, and I went to see his parents to wish them a happy new year. Back home, we had just finished dinner and he was in the kitchen while I was in the living room. The text alert rang out on his mobile, both our phones had been pretty quiet all day and I just asked:

'Oh, who's that?'

My husband didn't reply and so I asked again, and he stuttered something about it being junk. The hackles rose on the back of my neck. I couldn't explain why but something within me sensed that he was up to his old tricks again. As usual, he needed to be awake early for work but this time he left both of his mobile phones downstairs with me to charge up!

I waited until I heard the safety of his snores, and not being able to help myself, I checked both of his phones. There it was as plain as day. More text messages and emails from gay dating websites. I was furious and after our frank and honest discussion about our marriage only two days before, I was heartbroken.

The anger took over my other emotions and I stormed upstairs into the bedroom with both of his phones in hand. It seemed like déjà vu. I threw open the door, shouting obscenities. He awoke instantly and sat bolt upright. I threw his phones at him and yelled that I knew what he had been up to again. He tried to say that he was sorry and that he loved me, but this time I'd had enough. I stormed into the other bedroom, packed a holdall full of clothes and I left him! Mum only lived a fifteen-minute walk away and so I called her to let her know that I was on my way. I told her I would explain the full story when I got there as it was after 9pm. My husband did follow me in the car, yelling at me to get in beside him so that we could talk. I simply told him to "drop dead."

Mum greeted me at her front door. I asked her to pour me a large drink before I told her why I had left my husband. I knocked most of the Martini straight back, I needed the Dutch courage to get the sorry mess off my chest! My mum and Stepdad were deeply shocked and utterly gobsmacked by everything that I told them. Mum was upset that I had stood by him for so long and that I had kept things to myself for all of that time. She did understand why when I explained the timings and that I had been so affected by everything else that I had chosen not to deal with it and ignore it to some degree.

Mum agreed that I could stay at her house, so the next couple of days were spent collecting my things from the house. Further discussions were held between my husband and I. Although I made it clear that things were over from my perspective, I admit that I wavered after he persuaded me that we could still be husband and wife but live apart and have our own lives. A very modern marriage, I suppose. Within twenty-four hours, I had discovered that was just a ruse to cover up the fact that he had opened new accounts on the gay dating websites. I broke it off permanently then.

I put a lot of my things into storage. As luck would have it, it was only necessary for a month. The landlady at the property where my husband and I had our first flat had another flat vacant to let. It was at a rent that I could afford on my own and it was perfect for me at the time. I moved in at the beginning of February. I loved being at mums, but I always needed my own space.

Over the coming months, many other events unfolded. The worst was being tested for an STD because my husband had called and informed me that he had tested positive for Chlamydia! He wasn't particularly forthcoming on when he had been infected either. My tests were all negative but as the results would take a while, I was prescribed antibiotics as a precaution when I explained the situation. I felt so bloody embarrassed, but it was just something else to add to the list by this point! I won a PPI case that had paid for our wedding. I used the money to pay for the divorce and a short holiday to Corfu in the summer of that year. People still chuckle when I tell them about this! My dad moved into sheltered accommodation where he could be better monitored.

That August, I turned thirty. I was a thirty-year-old divorcee with trust issues! I was hurting and I was bloody angry! My ex-husband was unable to admit his truth and kept telling the family that our split was my fault because I was "better organised than him!" The family knew what had happened when we got together so they didn't believe that as a story, and neither mum nor I were willing to cover for him anymore. Thanks to social media, we ended up outing him. I'm really not proud of this and washing my dirty linen in public isn't a good look for anyone, but he had put me through enough. It didn't help my sense of humiliation and shame. I felt like he had been conveniently using me as his cloak of normality rather than just being honest about his sexuality. I tried to remain friends with him but there would always be trust issues there for me even if he was my cousin, so we disconnected.

My next course of action admittedly wasn't the smartest, but I can only put it down to seeking some kind of revenge against my ex-husband. I wanted male company but clearly, I was in no state for a relationship, so I signed up to a couple of extra-marital dating sites. My thinking was very skewed, but I always took precautions, and I ended up sleeping with a few married men. I was shocked by their attitudes towards their wives and marriages, but I was in no position to judge, and I had now proved to be no better than my ex-husband.

I looked in the mirror and I didn't like the person staring back at me, so I stopped and resolved to stay single, or at least just see single men. I needed to cut some of the drama out of my life after all! I had started a degree, so I mostly concentrated on that and my job. At least my degree was something more positive! Of course, my fibromyalgia wasn't brilliant during these years. If I was sick from work, I was still at home doing my coursework!

As for cutting drama out of my life, I was off work with stress during the summer of 2012. As I began to feel better, I returned to work, but I needed a holiday. I booked a trip to Majorca, and it was just what I needed, and I felt recharged when I flew home.

Only two days after my return, my brother called, and we somehow ended up having an argument about things that one of mum's boyfriends had said to him years before. It included how he was treated and that it was all mum's fault. I don't know if it was because I was too relaxed from my holiday, but I snapped back without thinking:

'At least it was only words with you and nothing else!'

When Tez asked me what I had meant by that, I couldn't speak for a couple of moments because I realised what I had said.

'Do you mean that he touched you?' Tez asked.

I couldn't reply straightaway. I had kept the secret of my abuse for so damn long and I couldn't help but wonder why the hell I had let it slip now? Eventually, I began to speak, and I told my brother that I had been abused by the particular person he had been crying about from the ages of 13 to 16. Tez didn't take it too well, he started shouting about mum being a bad mother and that it was all her fault. I tried to explain that mum didn't know a damn thing about my abuse, but he hung up. I realised then that I was crying, and I was beginning to shake.

I couldn't think, my brother knew my secret and he was angry. I knew that he was going to call mum. I resolved to try and beat him to it, but her mobile number was engaged, and she didn't have voicemail. I began to pace around the flat wringing my hands and feeling panicked. Eventually, my mobile rang. I jumped because it was mum. I answered and she was in floods of tears. She had spoken to Tez, and she asked me if it was true what he had told her about the abuse. I told her that it was, and mum began to cry even harder. I told her that it wasn't her fault and that my abuser had threatened to hurt Tez if I said or did anything.

Mum asked me to go to her house immediately so, I agreed. I rushed around the flat packing things into my small suitcase, I figured that I may as well stay for the weekend. My brain was rushing all over the place, I was panicking that mum wouldn't believe me. I didn't want to face my brother. I don't know why but I called the only other person in the world that I had told, my ex-husband! To be fair to him, he was rather sweet about it, and he wished me well. Apparently, he even called my mum whilst I was enroute to her house to explain more to her which I was grateful for.

I reached mum's house about an hour later and my brother was already there with a face like thunder. Mum was still crying, and my stepdad just held out his arms and enveloped me in a massive hug. I collapsed into them and sobbed for a good long while before mum got up and took me into her arms and we had a good long hug too. Eventually, a little calmer, we all sat down, and I explained everything that had happened to me at the hands of my abuser all those years ago. I felt a sense of relief yet, a sense of shame that I had kept it hidden for so long. I just didn't know how to start that conversation. I was already seeing a counsellor for CBT to help me manage stress, but mum wanted me to speak to someone more specialised.

She could see just how big a weight carrying

all of that was with everything else on top. I agreed to have a chat with my counsellor at my next session. My brother was devastated. He apologised for making it all about him, but he acknowledged that he wasn't coping well with the news. I was grateful for the apology as was mum, as his anger towards her had by all accounts been pretty intense, but I didn't know what to say to him. I couldn't undo what I had told him, I couldn't undo the fact that the abuse had happened and that I had kept it quiet for almost fifteen years by this point. I had to let him go home and deal with things in his own way, I needed to concentrate on me. I knew that I needed help and I wanted so badly to reassure mum and try to take away some of her hurt. I am still working on that one many years later!

After a fairly intense weekend, I returned to work, and I had a counselling session that afternoon too. What a Monday! My counsellor was able to provide me with contact details for a local organisation that offered counselling to those who had been sexually abused as children and were now adults. I made contact as soon as I reached home. They called me for an assessment appointment a few days later. I had to wait a few weeks to see an actual counsellor, but I was still undergoing the CBT therapy anyway. My boss at work noticed that I had seemed a bit withdrawn that week. I couldn't tell her everything, I just hinted that something bad in my past had come up again recently and we needed time to deal with things as a family and she was satisfied with that as she didn't want to pry.

Me being me, I carried on managing life and dad was a part of that. His Alzheimer's was progressing, and things were getting more and more difficult. He began to leave the house less and less so my brother and I would go to the flat to visit him. We tried to encourage him to go to day care centres and meet other people in a similar situation to him. He went twice and blatantly refused to go again and trying to change the mind of a man who has bi-polar disorder and Alzheimer's is quite frankly impossible, so we gave up trying fairly quickly! The sheltered accommodation block where dad lived was next door to a pub. He only actually set foot in that pub twice the entire time that he lived there. A few years before that, he would have absolutely loved living there!

Eventually, I began attending my specialist counselling appointments. I kind of enjoyed my appointments, as they were my time to discuss exactly what was on my mind and work things through. It always felt strange realising that not everyone thinks the way that I do about certain things! Having to unlearn my thinking having been hurt so badly was especially hard.

My counsellor did point out that I had been

hurt by practically every single man that had ever come into my life by that point! It really was no wonder that my thinking about love, relationships, men, and life in general, was so screwed up! I went for counselling for about nine months in total, I liked my counsellor and the centre always felt like such a safe space. By the end of the sessions, I was in a place, mentally, where I felt like I could trust myself and look after myself again and on my own terms.

Whilst I was looking after myself and feeling good, I did turn inwardly a bit more. I became a hermit outside of work! I left home to go to work and to university and that was pretty much it. I was happy in my own company studying, watching TV or cooking. I did socialise occasionally, but I had a tendency to overdo it on the alcohol, so I didn't do it too often. I didn't like drunk people when I was sober, so I always had an "if I can't beat em, join em" attitude. And join them I usually did - gaining a massive weekend hangover for my troubles.

In July 2014, I graduated with a 2:1 from my university course. I was so proud but relieved that my course was over. I had faced so many trials all whilst trying to study and work at the same time that I felt like I needed a breather. It began to dawn on me though that I could use my degree to change my career, but I got angry at my situation. I couldn't just leave dad, could I?

My brother had managed to take a massive step back from dad as he had a family to look after as a father of two young boys. This began to stew for a while and eventually, I decided that I was going to apply to do some postgraduate courses out of Leicester. Unfortunately, I couldn't gain the funding that I needed, and my PhD proposal really needed more work than I could commit or focus on. I decided to just accept my lot, I had a part time job with a full-time salary, and I had a roof over my head. Anyone who has a long-term chronic illness will tell you the aftereffects of a decision like this! I was ill a lot of the time through stress. I hated my job; my dad was dependent on me and in all honesty, I just struggled to cope.

Chapter Nine - And so, it continued!

By the following month, my brother's relationship had fallen apart, and I agreed to let him move in with me. He lived with me for six months, sleeping on a mattress on my living room floor as my flat only had one bedroom. Dad was in and out of hospital for various reasons but mostly involving him having had a fall. Eventually, dad agreed to look at care homes as social services had gotten involved. Luckily, there was a space at the care home across the road from my flat and he moved in there. Because dad had been sectioned whilst having Alzheimer's, social services funded his care home fees. We were grateful for that as whilst dad had some money, it wouldn't have taken long for this to be swallowed up if he had to pay the fees.

Tez had moved out into his own flat and had a new girlfriend so I would pop across the road to see dad most weekends. It was hard to witness his decline, occasionally he wouldn't really be there, even though he was sat in front of me, so I didn't stay for long. I wasn't happy at my flat, I wanted somewhere a bit bigger as it felt really tiny and cold and so I began to search for my next home. I had been there four and a half years and I hadn't meant to stay for that long, but it was the safety net and bolthole that I had needed after my separation and then divorce.

I found a lovely flat just outside the city which I fell in love with. I had been moved in only a matter of days when I was rudely awoken at 4.30am. I was on the ground floor and the noise was coming from my upstairs neighbour. After chatting to another neighbour, I was told that the lady upstairs had just returned from a holiday to her home country of Poland. Every morning at 4.30am, I could hear her clomping around her flat above my head! I could never go back to sleep properly, and I actually have no idea how I got to work some days because I was so exhausted! One day, some of her post was delivered to me by mistake so I took my opportunity to pop upstairs and meet her in person. She was not what I expected. She was smaller than me. I could not understand how this little woman made so much bloody noise!

A noisy neighbour wasn't the only issue with my flat, it turned out that there was a rising damp problem! The back of the leather sofa which came with the flat regularly grew a thick green furry coat. Mum would regularly come to my house to help me scrub it off with bleach. I complained to the landlord who fobbed me off by purchasing a dehumidifier because "old houses breathed differently!" Every day, I would come home from work and empty out more than a litre of water from the machine. I couldn't properly check for damp because the carpets had been glued down, I later learnt that was a suspicious thing to do.

I also found black mould in the wardrobe that again had come with the flat. After six months of being woken up at 4.30am and the mould, I decided that I'd had enough! I began to look for somewhere else to live so that I did not need to sign another six-month lease.

My health was massively affected by everything. I 'd lost a lot of weight and everything that I ate was making me ill. The doctor had referred me for a gastroscopy at the hospital to see if they could find out what was happening with my stomach, but they hadn't found out anything. Dad was going downhill, and the care home informed me that his building society had decided that he no longer had the capability to conduct his financial affairs.

I was in agreement and so were the Department for Work and Pensions when they conducted their visit to assess his capability. It was decided that I would take over dad's finances. A man from the DWP visited me and we completed the forms, I set up a bank account solely for dad's money to be paid into and I paid his bills from that. I tried to see dad as often as I could, but I was often too unwell due to my digestive problems.

During my search for somewhere to live that was closer to my mum and stepdad, which was my original intention, I found a gorgeous quarter house about ten minutes' walk from mum's. I loved it and I signed all the paperwork straight away and I set a moving date for the end of January 2016. Work weren't entirely pleased with me booking a week's holiday during the semester one exam period but they had seen me over the previous six months and how tired that I had been and so understood my need to move.

It was lovely being so close to mum and there were many invites for Sunday dinners! Tez was doing better and had a girlfriend who he was moving to Hull with as that was her latest posting.

Sadly, dad declined further, and I was regularly receiving calls from his care home that he had been taken to hospital. As I was the closest sibling now geographically, I would rush to be by his bedside. He worried me sick, twice he had been unresponsive, and it wasn't until he reached the hospital that they would be able to rouse him. The hospital conducted MRI scans and they were never able to ascertain what had happened.

They did suspect mini strokes, but they just could not tell. Weirdly though, it was like dad had received a jolt to the brain because once he was awake, he was lucid, talkative and knew exactly what was going on and who I was. He would spend a day or two in hospital and then he would be discharged back to the care home. With dad suffering from both bipolar disorder and Alzheimer's though, he would become so frightened and paranoid of what was going on, often gripping on to me for dear life so hard that he nearly broke my fingers twice!

Then things with dad really began to take a downward turn when he contracted sepsis twice. The first time, I was terrified that I was going to lose him as it didn't appear that the antibiotics were working. The nurses sent me home to get some rest late on a Sunday evening. I left with a heavy heart.

I returned on the Monday morning with mum. We were utterly dumbstruck to find him sat up in bed laughing and eating his cornflakes! However, later that day, dad's mental health issues kicked in. He became fixated on death and the shadow of death, and he kept talking about something to do with black lace and not making a great deal of sense. Mum and I spent the entire afternoon trying to settle him to sleep, eventually at about 5pm, he finally gave in! We decided that we should go home and get some food. On our way out of the ward we saw a vicar dressed in the usual black shirt and dog collar going in. Dad wasn't religious but we were terrified of dad waking up and seeing the vicar after his paranoid delusions all afternoon and so we waited to see which direction the vicar went in and luckily, he didn't go near dad's section of the ward.

My health was still all over the place and

the doctors asked me to begin eating wheat again as I had previously stopped in the belief that I may be coeliac. My blood results appeared to confirm this when they rose whilst I was eating wheat and they declined sharply when I stopped. The specialist at the hospital said that whilst the results from the gastroscopy were inconclusive, the blood results meant that I would be treated as a coeliac patient. I was advised to stop eating wheat and anything else containing gluten immediately and I was referred to an education workshop and to the dietitian to help me gain some weight back. I'd become a very skinny size ten and whilst most people would be overjoyed to have lost three stone and four dress sizes, I felt so wrong and uncomfortable within my body and self.

After that, I basically ate a gluten free diet and whatever else I could manage without feeling ill, as I apparently still had a whole lot of other food allergies. Again, dad was rushed into hospital with suspected sepsis, this time due to the catheter that had been inserted during his last admission to hospital. It had been deemed clinically necessary to send him back to the home with it. I was furious as he was vulnerable to bladder infections anyway, he didn't need a catheter to make things more difficult.

Luckily, this infection wasn't too severe, but the doctor did say to me when she first visited dad, that given his weight loss and how his dementia was progressing, it was likely that he was in the last year of life. I didn't need to hear that, and it was a hard conversation to have with my brother while he was living all the way up in Hull. He visited when he could if he was collecting his sons for the weekend, but it was mostly all on my shoulders. I literally had no choice but to accept things and carry on. I had mum for support and hugs, but I lived on my own and it was me who received the calls when dad was rushed to the hospital. I began to struggle with the responsibility and the state of my health combined.

I argued with the doctors at the hospital to get the catheter removed and it took about two more weeks for the appointment to come through from outpatients. The care home understood my anger over it and were in support of it being removed. But it was me that the hospital was willing to listen to, not their care staff who see the outcome of the infections more often than me!

But about two weeks after that catheter had been removed, dad wasn't right again. I had a Friday off of work and I went to the care home. Dad confused me with my brother, and he was hardly eating or drinking again, and he had a chesty cough and was clearly struggling. The next day, I had gone shopping with mum to a local town and we were having a lovely day. We had just finished lunch at a pub when my phone rang, it was the care home. They had just sent dad to casualty in an ambulance and this time they were adamant that it was sepsis. Mum and I rushed to the hospital on the bus. That bus ride felt like the longest ever ride I can tell you! I was scared this time, having seen him the day before. A part of me just knew that something big was coming!

We arrived at the hospital, worried about what we would find. Dad was fairly non-responsive, but he knew my mum and kissed the back of her hands! That still breaks my heart to this day. Eventually we were moved to a ward and the doctor came to see dad who was now unconscious again. The doctor asked to talk to me privately. I asked if mum could join us as I just knew that this conversation was not going to be easy.

He gently told us that dad wasn't responding to the antibiotics this time and that there were two options. Give him one last big shot of antibiotics and hope that they work, or we could let him gently slip away as he wasn't getting any better, he was getting thinner, and the quality of his life was a consideration that we needed to make. I told him that it wasn't a decision that I could make alone, I needed to call my brother.

Tez was devastated when I called but he wasn't willing to discuss it over the phone. He and his girlfriend would drive down from Hull straightaway. I agreed that it was probably the best thing and so I asked the doctor to keep dad comfortable for the time being. We sat by dad's bedside watching dad's heart monitor for three hours until Tez arrived. The monitor showed that dad's heart rate was incredibly erratic, he wasn't conscious and needed oxygen to breathe.

It was very late in the evening when eventually Tez arrived with his girlfriend. I never even asked the nursing staff if we could stay with Dad, I assumed they understood how bad things were and that it wasn't an issue. Tez and I went to another room that was set aside for relatives to sit and discuss our options. He used to be a healthcare assistant, so he had some understanding of the situation. We both agreed that given dad's quality of life and the number of hospital visits that dad had made over recent months and that things were just getting worse, it would be kinder to let him slip away.

It was the hardest decision that we had ever made and neither of us took it very well. I fetched the doctor and told him our decision. The nurses disconnected the heart machine, and they gave him an injection of morphine for pain relief. We took it in turns to sit with dad over the next thirty-six hours so that he wasn't alone.

At around 2am on the second night in hospital, the four of us were sat with Dad as he was still hanging on. Suddenly dad's eyes flicked open! He began to shake all over, his hands and legs were everywhere, and I ran to fetch the nurse. They gave him something to help him to relax. He wasn't really awake. We were all in pieces as it had shaken us all up. Tez and his girlfriend drove back to mum's so that they could get some sleep whilst mum and I remained at dad's side. I was adamant that I wasn't leaving dad alone as I knew that his death was close. As I had held his hand, I literally felt his soul slipping away, or at least that was how I felt at the time.

Mum and I fell asleep at dad's bedside. I awoke at 7.30am and I noticed that his Adam's apple wasn't moving up and down as much as it previously had been. I knew in my heart that he was really going this time. I woke mum up and we called Tez. It was becoming clear that there was not enough time for Tez to get back to the hospital. Some of the night staff from dad's care home arrived, they had grown quite fond of dad in his time as a resident and they wanted to say their goodbyes.

They hadn't been at the hospital more than half an hour when dad passed away. Mum held his hand as I stroked his forehead. We called Tez to let him know what was happening and apparently, he immediately ran to the toilet to vomit. Mum and I held each other and sobbed. We all sat with dad and talked for a while, but he couldn't be part of the conversation anymore.

Over the coming days, we took care of the necessary arrangements and administration of everything there is to do when you lose a loved one. The hardest part was having to keep saying to someone new 'our dad has died.' By the end of the week, we had the funeral organised, the wake was going to be held at one of dad's favourite pubs, this was important to me and Tez, and his room had been cleared out at the home. The care staff were all very kind, they all thought a lot of our dad which meant a lot to both of us, and they told us some stories that made us laugh.

I had taken the week off work as compassionate leave, but I returned to work at the beginning of the following week. I lasted one whole day at work, and I nearly left many times before that. I couldn't cope anymore, I got home and I just broke, there was still a few more days before the funeral. I couldn't imagine carrying on with life during what felt like a 'limbo phase.' I hadn't yet said a final goodbye to dad, I wasn't ready to allow my life to carry on and think about work - it all felt pointless. I took some more time off on official sick leave thanks to a very understanding GP.

The funeral was hard on both Tez and I. Neither of us were used to public speaking but we were both adamant that we wanted to speak and say our own proper goodbyes. Tez did a re-imagined version of *Stop the Clock* by WH Auden, and I had written a speech. We both cried a lot, but we had each other to lean on as well as other members of the family who attended. I had a good few drinks at the wake, I didn't know how to get through things any other way - I am my father's daughter after all!

In the coming days, Tez and his girlfriend returned home to Hull, and I tried to go back to work again. I managed to get to the end of the week, but I was crying a lot either in the toilet or when I got home after keeping it together all day. Because of the amount of time that I had taken off due to sickness over the year, I needed to make an appointment to see the Doctor and get signed off sick officially.

Luckily, she was very kind and we discussed various options and we agreed for me to start on a low dose of an antidepressant. She also referred me for some Cognitive Behavioural Therapy to help with the stress that I had communicated to her previously. She was concerned that I had been exhibiting physical symptoms of anxiety in the previous months and it wasn't a surprise that she said this looking back.

With all that had been going on with dad, I had been a mess. Now that he was gone, I didn't feel like I knew who I was and what I was doing moving forward. I couldn't cope with the simplest of things and my emotions were all over the place. It was also my thirty fifth Birthday. I didn't do anything beyond go round to mum's and spend time there, I didn't want to be on my own, but I wasn't ready to celebrate anything, and I had just been given a prescription of anti-depressants on my birthday!

I discovered just how big a problem I had with death and cremations when we collected dad's ashes from the funeral home. I totally fell apart and my stepdad had to practically hold me up as I collapsed in his arms when we reached mum's house. Thankfully Tez decided to take dad's ashes home until we decided to scatter his ashes. We scattered dad's ashes in Skegness as per his wishes about a month after dad's funeral. The lifeboat crew agreed to scatter them off the coast for us as this was something they did regularly for other people apparently. We both cried bucket loads as this was the final goodbye.

In total, I spent around three months on sick leave as my anxiety ramped up as well as the depression that continued to lurk. Some days, I could barely leave the house or get out of bed. In time, I began to get better but progress was slow I must admit. My brother and his girlfriend went on holiday to Cornwall with his two boys for a week and they needed someone to look after their cat so I said that she could come and stay with me for a week. I fell in love with her and appreciated having her around the house, she gave me a reason to get up in the morning if only to feed her. mum had an idea; she had lost a cat within the last year, and she saw an advertisement online for a pair of kittens.

One was a boy, and one was a girl. Mum wanted us to have one kitten each, I wanted the boy, and she wanted the girl, so my Stepdad took us to see them. We both fell in love and brought them home right away. Mum looked after my kitten until my house guest had returned home. I named my kitten Benji, he was black and white and very playful and pretty independent too. Having a kitten in the house full time was a steep learning curve for me, I'd had cats before but now I was totally responsible for him. I adored him and he liked to sleep on my bed at night and he would lie down on his back for a belly rub when I had been out anywhere.

Chapter Ten - Things begin to change (at last!)

After a few weeks of just me and Benji, I felt well enough to return to work. Benji and I settled into a routine, but I couldn't quite settle back at work. I was on a slow phased return, and I was starting back at zero as I had been away for such a long time or so it seemed. I was still anxious and some days it did all get too much and no matter how hard I tried, I couldn't stop crying and I couldn't leave the house!

Sadly, my boss didn't understand my condition particularly well and she told me that I had a duty to come to work! I understood that and I still do, but mental health is mental health, and I didn't have any coping mechanisms and I could not shake it off. To be honest, the harder that I tried, the worse I began to feel, and it was just exhausting. Eventually though, the appointments for the CBT came through. It helped at the time, but this therapy isn't something that I have ever managed to keep in my consciousness on a regular basis as a toolkit to help during a bad time.

What I had begun to realise though was that I had a lot of 'work friends' but no one that I really saw outside of work, and I realised that I needed some real human connections in my life. I had heard about a site and an app called *Meetup* and there was a group who met in Leicester City Centre and the focus was centred on goals and achieving things. I decided that this was something that I definitely needed and so I went along to their first meeting of 2017. I am pleased to say that I am still friends with people that I met at this group. They were warm and understood what I had been through, and they were encouraging.

Through this group who usually met monthly, I began to write a book that I had the idea for a few years before. I decided that I was going to learn to drive as I had some inheritance money from dad and one of the members was a driving instructor. I began to socialise at other events and enjoyed nights out with this crowd of good-hearted people.

The universe had other nice surprises in store for me too it seems. In May of 2017, my mum was celebrating her birthday with a group of people that she knew from the charity shop where she was working. I was sat next to one of the guys who was a part-time volunteer. He had me laughing most of the night until he went home. Over the coming days, it transpired that mum, and the Shop Manager were having conversations about setting us up on a date!

My number was given to Terry, and he called me a couple of days after we first met. We spent five hours on the phone in total and we laughed a lot. He was eighteen years older than me but honestly that did not bother me a jot. It has become clear that age gap relationships run through my family like seaside rock!

We arranged to meet for a drink and dinner at the end of that week and we continued to speak on the phone and text during the week. I was quite nervous; I knew that I was beginning to feel something for this man, and I wasn't sure if I could trust myself or my instincts. My friend had a cunning plan though, I told her which shop he worked in, and she decided to go and check him out and let me know what she thought. Terry was given her seal of approval and she told me to go for it! We met and again, there were a lot of laughs, but I held back from taking any action and it was clear that he hadn't realised that we were on a date. I wasn't sure if he was looking for friendship or something else?

However, we continued to chat on the phone a lot and there was a lot of chemistry, at least in my mind! I grew impatient and I invited him along to my friend's birthday drinks which took place the week after our first meal. Luckily, she was more than happy for him to come along!

Things went well, he got on with my friends and as we left the pub, I grabbed his hand, and he kept hold of it as we walked back to the bus station. We said goodbye to my friends, and they made their way to their individual bus stops and then we were left alone. I decided to take the bull by the horns as I got the impression that he was being quite shy, so I kissed him. He responded and we have been a couple ever since!

We grew very close quite quickly and it wasn't long before things progressed, and we began living together within about three months. I honestly could not be happier in our relationship - Terry is unlike any other man that I have known. He is kind, supportive, funny, and loving. He has had mental health issues too, so he understands me when I am struggling whether that be mentally or physically, because my fibromyalgia is causing pain or discomfort. I could not be more grateful to my mum and the Shop Manager for setting us up to exchange numbers. We know that you set us up and we were both told different things, but we don't hold it against you!

A few months later, I was still unhappy with my job and the stress was not doing my anxiety any good at all. During a conversation with a friend about my future career plans, counselling was mentioned again. A few people had said that I would make a good counsellor because I like to talk to people and to help them to feel better.

I knew that this wasn't exactly what I wanted to do though and then my friend mentioned life coaching. I was intrigued so I booked onto a weekend with a provider who ran a free foundation course to introduce people to what the full life coaching qualification would entail. I was sold and I realised that this was what I wanted to do.

Life coaching can fit into so many areas of life and help people to move forward with so many different things. I signed up as soon as I got home. I resolved to sort out the situation at work and now I had a purpose, and I knew that I didn't want to remain there anymore. I had some money in the bank which would cover the cost of the course and living expenses for a period of time. I just could not cope anymore, and work agreed to allow me to hand in my notice, and with my holiday entitlement I was able to leave at the end of that week before the Christmas holiday. I was sorry to leave some of my work colleagues, I had worked with them for nine years and they had seen me go through a lot, but the job had become more stressful, and I needed to look after myself and my health.

For Christmas 2017, I paid for myself, my mum and Stepdad to stay at a cottage in Sheringham as mum had always had a wish to be at the seaside for Christmas. The cottage was beautiful and of course Terry came along with us. It was a lovely Christmas and knowing that I wasn't going back to work really did help me to feel so much more positive than I had in a long time.

I went straight into my life coach training, and I loved it. I needed to do some actual live coaching so a few of my friends volunteered themselves as clients and other life coaching trainees became my sample clients and I became theirs. The world of personal development and accountability really gave me the impetus to address some of my other goals.

As I wasn't working, I had time to finish the book that I had begun to write the previous year. I did try to get it published but the only publishers that were interested were vanity publishers who wanted me to pay £3K to get it published and they wouldn't do a lot of work to sell any of my books because they had already made their money. I am proud to report that I have recently self-published this novel as an ebook.

I completed my driving lessons and passed in August 2018, and I bought my first car. I enjoyed accomplishing things and I enjoyed seeing my clients accomplish their goals too. I gained my life coaching qualification in early 2019. It was the best thing that I ever did, and I look forward to working with clients in the near future.

The last couple of years, I have been working for a local charity in HR and this has since led to forays into my own business as a self-employed HR Assistant contractor for another. Being self-employed does give me a lot of flexibility and I enjoy that immensely.

During 2020, a friend's son was struggling with his career direction and so I offered to give him a coaching session centred on DISC

Personality testing. We both got a lot from that one session, and I realised that coaching is what I am meant to do with my life, so I am now working towards setting up my own coaching business. After all that I have been through, I am empathetic, and I am a positive coach always cheerleading my clients forward on their goals.

My life tips

I am more than happy to acknowledge that what you have been through is likely to be wildly different to my story but if you have read this far, perhaps you may find something here for you.

Therapy

This is absolutely vital to deal with your past. It is a safe space, where you will not be judged for anything that you say or feel and it is perfectly okay to be in therapy, it really is. I do wish now that I had gone along to grief counselling when dad passed away, but I dealt with things in my own way. It can be a little tricky to find the right therapy for the situation that you need but I do highly recommend person-centred therapy. It really does help just to talk all of your shit out and your counsellor can often help you to see things from another perspective. During counselling for my sexual abuse – the analogy of the bag and what you have to or choose not to carry around with you has always stuck with me.

GP/Doctors

Never, ever, ever be ashamed to ask for help! If you are suffering and you need medication for a short period or a long time, take the bloody tablets, there is no shame in needing them and attend ALL your appointments. In the media especially, there is a lot of negativity against taking medication but think of your brain as an electric circuit board, sometimes there is a break in the circuit, and you may need the medication to bridge the break in that circuit. If you were physically sick and you needed the medication, you would take it wouldn't you? Mental health is just the same.

Forgiveness and letting go

Forgive yourself for the past. I now know that much of my past wasn't my fault. I was a child who was manipulated into keeping secrets from my loved ones and I grew up into a confused and angry adult who made bad choices due to all of the various traumas. Journaling can be of help here, write out how you feel about who hurt you and how they hurt you. You don't ever have to look at this again and you could burn those pieces of paper and feel that bad energy leave you! Let go of things that aren't serving you. I realised that there has been a pattern of drama and I attracted it. Now if I don't have to get involved I won't. My physical and mental health is much more important. You could try a cord-cutting meditation to help with this, do a search on YouTube for these and find one that sits right with you.

Shame

Don't feel ashamed for the trauma that you have been through, own it and acknowledge it but most of all TALK ABOUT IT! The more that you do, the easier and less scary it will become for you. Hanging onto that shame I feel has cost me dearly in terms of both my physical and mental health. It has taken time to improve my mental health certainly and fibromyalgia will always be with me. I believe that we need to talk about the tough stuff to break the stigma, help people to understand and generally allow ourselves to heal from the shit. I have to remember when I talk about my abuse that other people are so shocked it is because it is the first time that they are hearing about it and for me this is old news. Some people have thought that I have been a little clinical when talking about it. I think it is because I am so over it now that talking about it doesn't affect me anymore.

Honesty

Be honest about how you are feeling. People might not always understand the effects of trauma or mental health, but I am all about BREAKING THE STIGMA and opening up the conversation. I know people use this expression a lot, but it is okay not to be okay. People need to be made aware and made to understand. I once had a boss who didn't understand how my mental health was affecting me and during one particular episode when I couldn't leave the house because I didn't feel safe, she told me that I had "a duty to come to work!" I was very aware of that, but mental health is mental health and people need to be more understanding and you need to never ever feel ashamed for having an illness whether it be physical or mental.

Friendships

I didn't have many real friends, only work colleagues who were brilliant, but you need friends who you can count on outside of work. Join meetup or join hobby or craft groups to meet like-minded people. Your tribe are out there, and yes online friends can help. But, it will help you immensely to find friendships where you can leave the damn house to socialise and don't become a hermit! You may surprise yourself and other people will be just as nervous as you but having friends is good for you and your mental health.

Goals

Have a goal, no matter how small! I started driving lessons and writing a fictional book. It still needs a little work before it can be self-published, but it will be done, I swear! Even if your goal is to get dressed that day, it is something to aim for and achieve, please don't give up trying! My mum always tells me that "all good things come to those who wait," I am sorry mum, but sometimes you've got to go and get it for yourself! I have included an exercise at the end of the book, which is a great starting point for goal setting called the Be, Do, Have exercise. When you have worked out what your goals are and if you would like to work with me, my contact details are also at the end of the book.

Be realistic

If you want to make big changes to your life, it's important to have the love and support of those around you. If you are in a relationship and you need time to do something, discuss what needs to be done around the house and compromise occasionally. If you need to let go of being Mrs Hinch and living in a show home then just do what is absolutely necessary!

Acceptance

Accept that you won't get things right every time and that sometimes you will have mental and/or physical health conditions to deal with. I still have my bad days, I'm not perfect and that's perfectly okay. Don't accept the default and settle for a life that you don't want or that makes you feel unhappy. Make that shift in mindset and your identity – again I can help you with this through my coaching!

Relationships

Don't ignore those red flags, no matter how small. Looking back, I know that I should have left my ex-husband sooner or maybe not even married him at all. I was ashamed and exhausted by the whole situation and in all honesty, I don't recognise that woman anymore. I recommend reading *The Gift of Fear* if you sometimes feel that you are too accommodating in relationships or too nice for your own good!

Talk about money! Yes, it is a hard conversation but honestly this is a biggie and causes so much resentment if you can't discuss it. Terry and I are able to have proper discussions about money like adults without arguing, honestly this was a revelation to me as I never got anywhere with my ex-husband – it only led to bickering and silence! If they won't discuss money like a grown up, I urge you to walk away!

Important Stuff!

Live life for you! Know your own self-worth. What is right for you, is right for you. No-one else and their opinion matters! Love yourself enough not to compromise and accept second best anymore. And I will also say in the age of social media ignore the trolls! Block, delete and move on. It doesn't matter who these people are to you, you do not have to put up with that level of negativity and shit!

Be, Do, Have Activity

I recommend doing this in your journal or a notebook so that you can come back to this later!

We are going to explore everything that you want to do, be or have. This will assist you to set short, medium, and long-term goals.

Make sure that you are able to devote ample *thinking time* to each stage highlighted below.

Stage 1

Write down all the things that you want to BE, DO or HAVE

Stage 2

Write in one brief sentence **why** you want to BE, DO, HAVE each item on your list. If you can't do this with any of them, cross them off your list.

Stage 3

Decide the most important areas of your life – for example and in no particular order…

- Family
- Friends
- Career/Work
- Financial
- Health & Vitality
- Emotional well-being
- Social life

- Fun & recreation
- Physical environment (where and how you are living and your surroundings)
- Spiritual life

Add change or delete to include all the areas of life that are important to you. Define what success means to you in each of the life areas you have identified.

Stage 4

Take each of your goals in turn and ask the question:

Will having, being or doing this thing improve the areas of my life that I deem are important? Give one mark for each *Yes* answer.

Stage 5

For each of your goals, ask if it is right and fair to everyone in my sphere of influence and concern and if it will take you closer to your overall objective.

Stage 6

Put your goals in order. Take your top 10 goals. These are the ones that you are going to work on first.

Define your goals into 4 main groups:

- Ongoing goals needing daily input
- Short-term goals to achieve within a week to a month
- Medium-term goals that may take

between a month and a year
- Long-term goals that may take longer than a year.

Stage 7

For each of the goals on the list, expand your **WHY**. Explain to yourself fully why you want to have this goal and what it will mean to you. Write this down.

Stage 8

Take each goal in turn and make 2 'to do' lists for each to show:
- What you are prepared to do to achieve it
- What you will need to do to achieve it.

Stage 9

Make a list of:
- The people you need to work with or
- The people who can help you
- The skills you might need to develop
- The actions you need to take
- What you need to learn
- What you need to understand.

Stage 10

Complete the rocking-chair test. Take yourself out into the future as age 82. Imagine a wonderful life you have designed for yourself. **Take a moment to close your eyes and visualise**

it. Feel it, hear what has happened within your amazing life, who was there, where were you?

Write down the story of your incredible life, the amazing things you've done, fantastic things you've seen, the people you have touched and the changes you have made in your own life.

Place your goals with their action points, within a timeframe. Put a start and finish date on them. **Remember a goal is a dream with a date!!**

Why have I written this book?

I honestly don't want anyone to ever feel like they are the only ones in life who are suffering. So many of us have been there and continue to go there. I know what it is like to go through shit and feel like you are clinging onto life by your fingernails. I want this book to give you hope and comfort that life can get better. It may not go back to what you are expecting or become the fantasy that you have spent so long building in your head, but it can be better than it has been and that is great and an achievement in itself!

BOOKS BY THIS AUTHOR

Trial By Tv

Aidan Grant hosts a TV show that has changed dramatically over the years. He thought he was helping people in the beginning, but now it has all become about ratings and launching new so called reality stars to humiliate for the public's viewing pleasures! It has totally snowballed from how it started!

BUT, thanks to the Head of Network, Ricky's friendship with the Prime Minister, things are set to take a whole new darker turn! Ricky could be set to pay for his involvement by actually becoming the very first defendant on Trial by TV!

Can Aidan help Ricky and prevent his show from being dragged into this car crash?

Printed in Great Britain
by Amazon